A LIFE OF NAPOLEON

A LIFE OF
NAPOLEON

by Stendhal

1956

THE RODALE PRESS

This translation first published in 1956
by The Rodale Press, 123 New Bond Street, London, W.1
and Rodale Books Inc., Emmaus, Pennsylvania
Printed and bound in England
by Mackays of Chatham

CONTENTS

INTRODUCTION

'On May 15th, 1796, General Bonaparte entered Milan at the head of that young army which had shortly before crossed the Bridge of Lodi and taught the world that after all these centuries Caesar and Alexander had a successor.'

This is the opening sentence of one of the world's greatest novels, written in Italy by a French consul and published in 1839 —Stendhal's *La Chartreuse de Parme*. In that beginning there is the echo of another book by Stendhal, written more than twenty years earlier, a *Life of Napoleon* which was not published until after his death.

The personality, motives, achievements and influence of men like Caesar, Alexander and Napoleon exert a limitless and permanent fascination; Napoleon most of all because his world and times are the nearest to us and the most easily understood. There is no end to the curiosity about him, to the distortion of the facts in books, the theatre and cinema, to the theorizing and romanticizing. Little corporal, great general, ruthless tyrant, brilliant legislator, vulgar Corsican upstart, in every rôle in which he is viewed there is basis for speculation and wonder. The century and a half which separate him from us are not the excuse for the lack of objective approach because, as Zola said, 'Napoleon's destiny was a hammer blow that cracked the brains of his times.' Napoleon's contemporaries found just as much difficulty in grasping the essentials of his character and the breadth of his influence as we have today. The *Journal* of General Gourgaud, who accompanied the deposed Emperor into exile on St. Helena, and the *Mémorial de Ste. Hélène* by Las Cases were written under the spell which Napoleon cast over his adherents, just as Sir Hudson Lowe's memoirs are filled with the critical reserve to be expected from the man responsible for the safe-keeping of Europe's most illustrious prisoner.

1

Stendhal, who lived through his rise, reign and fall, was fascinated by Napoleon and wrote in *Le Rouge et le Noir* that Julien Sorel had for many years never lived an hour without telling himself that 'Bonaparte, an obscure and penniless lieutenant, had made himself master of the world by his sword.' But Stendhal's *Life of Napoleon* is excitingly different from other contemporary biographies in conception, method of execution, and style.

Stendhal, born Henri Beyle in Grenoble in 1783, noted in 1802 his intention of writing three prose works, one on Napoleon, one on the Revolution, and one on the great men of the Revolutionary period. He added, with breathtaking calm and sureness of purpose, 'begin these works at the age of thirty-three, fifteen years from now.'

As a clerk in the War Office, Stendhal was posted to Milan during Napoleon's second Italian campaign. A cousin obtained for him a commission as second lieutenant in the Dragoons and he became A.D.C. to General Michaud. Despite the admiration with which he wrote of military life, Stendhal was neither an enthusiastic nor a brilliant soldier and he resigned his commission after a few months and returned to Paris. He was no more outstanding as playwright and business man and he returned to the army to take part in the Russian campaign as a non-combatant quartermaster-officer with the rank of Director-General of Reserve Supplies. He was very proud in later years of having taken part in the retreat from Moscow. He left the city on October 10th, 1812, and after forced marches and an attack by the Russians (he nevertheless managed to read a few pages each evening of a book by Madame du Deffand) he arrived in Paris on January 31st, 1813. Napoleon, he wrote, was not beaten by men but 'by his pride and the climate,' and he added in a foot-note, with his customary precision, that the winter had not set in early but, on the contrary, there was wonderful weather in Moscow on the day he left, with a frost of only three degrees and bright sunshine.

Stendhal never took part in a battle but, on his recall to the army after the retreat from Russia, he witnessed the battle of

Bautzen—'we had an excellent view, from noon until three, of everything that can be seen of a battle, which is to say nothing.' A quarter of a century later he used his impressions of Bautzen to describe Fabrice's participation in the battle of Waterloo in *La Chartreuse de Parme*. He went to Milan on sick leave after a bout of influenza and it was there, in 1817 and after the precise interval of fifteen years which he had planned, that he began his *Life of Napoleon*. Behind him he had his personal experience in the Grande Armée, the knowledge of Napoleon's final defeat, and France's rejection of her erstwhile leader. Stendhal read of Waterloo whilst in Venice and commented in his journal 'All is lost, even honour.'

He considered Napoleon's banishment to St. Helena to be a cruel and shameful action on England's part. He was reminded of Plutarch's heroes, he wrote at the end of the *Life*. When he visited Paris in 1817, for the first time in two years, he found the anti-Bonapartist reaction in full spate and he was disgusted by the way the French had turned against the general and Emperor whom they had idolized in the years when he led them to glory.

He found there were people still passionately interested in Napoleon. Byron, ' . . . a charming young man who looked eighteen although twenty-eight, with the profile of an angel . . .', plied him with questions about Napoleon and the Russian campaign as they strolled about the Scala in Milan.

In revolt against the denigration of Napoleon and conscious, as he talked about it, of the scope of the epic which he had witnessed, he translated an article on Napoleon from the *Edinburgh Review* and used it as the framework for his book, filling in with his own comments and with extracts from other books. He stated in his preface that there were 'two or three hundred authors . . . the editor has merely gathered together what he considered to be the right phrases.' He re-wrote much of what he borrowed and welded the book into something indubitably his. As the manuscript took shape he gave it to his friends and their pencilled remarks may still be seen on the draft in the Grenoble Municipal Library.

3

He dropped his work for six months and when he resumed it, on his return from Paris in the middle of 1818, he had before him Madame de Staël's *Considérations sur les principaux événements de la Révolution française*. He found it anti-Bonapartist and referred to it in his *Life of Napoleon* by saying that he wrote to refute a slander.

In 1821 Stendhal left Milan suddenly after having been watched by the Austrian police as a suspected French Government spy. He left *Napoleon* with a friend in Milan with whom it remained until Stendhal's death in 1842.

He did not forget his project, however, and almost twenty years later he set out to write an entirely new book entitled *Mémoires sur Napoleon* into which he introduced more personal anecdotes and passages copied from the books which had been published in the interval. This second manuscript remained unfinished and was sent to join the original *Life* in Milan.

When he was fifty-three Stendhal wrote 'My love for Napoleon is the only passion remaining to me; yet it does not prevent my seeing his faults and the petty weaknesses with which he can be reproached.' In this objective approach, in the study of details, and by the examination of the moral effect Napoleon exerted not only on the French but on the peoples he conquered, Stendhal inaugurated an entirely fresh historical method. His *Life of Napoleon* is an analytical record of the moral and ideological atmosphere of Napoleonic Europe as well as being a great writer's unforgettable portrait of one of the greatest men history has known, a portrait showing his weaknesses and failures as well as his grandeur and successes.

ROLAND GANT

4

PREFACE

Nam neque te regni summa ad fastigia, vexit Lucinae favor et nascendi inglorius ordo. Vivida sed belle virtus tutataque ferro Libertas.

ALDRICH, 1669, 50: 497.

THERE ARE SOME TWO OR THREE HUNDRED AUTHORS OF THIS *Life* in three hundred octavo pages. The editor has done no more than make a collection of those sentences which seemed to him to be to the point.

Since everyone has a definite idea about Napoleon, this *Life* cannot fully satisfy anyone. It is equally difficult to please one's readers by writing on subjects of either too little or too great an interest.

Each passing year will bring further clarifications; famous people will die and their memoirs will be published. What follows is an abstract of all that was known on the subject of Napoleon on February 1st, 1818.

Fifty years hence, the life of Napoleon will have to be re-written every year as and when the memoirs of Fouché, Lucien, Réal, Regnault, Caulaincourt, Sieyès, le Brun, and others, are published.

STENDHAL

[1]

What part of the inhabited world has not heard of the victories of this great man, and of the marvel of his life? They are related everywhere. Frenchmen who boast of them teach the foreigner nothing, and whatever I may say to you on the subject today, I shall, anticipating your thoughts, have to answer the silent reproach of having remained much inferior to my subject.

BOSSUET : *Funeral Oration on the Prince de Condé.*

I AM WRITING THIS LIFE OF NAPOLEON TO REFUTE A SLANDER. This is an unwise proceeding, because this slander has been spread abroad by the leading talent of the age, against a man who, for the past four years, has been exposed to the vengeance of all the powers on earth. I am restricted in the expression of my thoughts. I lack ability, and my noble adversary has the support of all the courts of summary jurisdiction. Furthermore, quite apart from her fame, this opponent enjoyed great wealth and possessed a considerable reputation in the salons of Europe, as well as all the social advantages. She flattered even the most humble names, and her posthumous fame will not fail to arouse the enthusiasm of all those noble writers who are ever ready to let themselves be moved by the misfortunes of those in authority, whatsoever their nature. The following summary is not, properly speaking, a *Life*—it is an historic account intended for the contemporary spectator of events.

Napoleon was born on August 15th, 1769, at Ajaccio to Charles Bonaparte and Letitia Ramolini. His father, who was not without ability, served under Paoli, and after the French had occupied the island of Corsica, he was several times Deputy of the nobility. The family originally came from Tuscany, principally from the little town of San Miniato where it had been established for several hundred years. The historian Mazzucchelli

7

mentions several Bonapartes who were distinguished men of letters. In 1796 there was still a Bonaparte living at San Miniato. This was a Chevalier Saint-Etienne, rich and much respected, who prided himself upon his connexion with the young conqueror of Italy. When Napoleon was powerful, sycophants discovered or invented proofs which made him a descendant of the Treviso tyrants of the Middle Ages. A claim probably as unfounded as that of those *émigrés* who sought to show that Napoleon came from the lowest ranks of the people. His elder sister was educated at Saint-Cyr; this fact alone proves that the Bonaparte family belonged to the old nobility.

In Italy, the name of Napoleon is a common one. It was one of the names adopted by the Orsini family, and it was introduced into the Bonaparte family through an alliance made during the sixteenth century, with the house of Lomellini.[1]

Count Marbeuf took over the command in Corsica and became attached to Madame Letitia Bonaparte. He procured Napoleon a place at the Brienne Military Academy which he entered when very young. There Napoleon distinguished himself by his gift for mathematics and by a singular love of reading. But he offended his teachers by the stubbornness with which he refused to learn Latin according to the accepted methods. In vain they tried to make him learn Latin verses and the primary rules by heart. He would never write Latin compositions or speak the language. To punish him for his obstinacy, he was kept at the school a year or two longer than the other pupils. He spent those years in silence and in solitude. He never joined in the games of his school-fellows. He never even spoke to them. Dreamy, silent, and solitary, he was known by his habit of imitating the manner of men of antiquity even to their language. He affected especially the short, sententious sentences of the Lacedaemonians. It is one of Europe's misfortunes that

[1] The following passage, from the *History of the House of Orsini* by Sansovino, may be of passing interest:
'Ma molti più furono i Napoleoni, perchè in tutti i tempi gli orecchi italiani, o nella pace, o nella guerra, udirono questo nobilissima voce in uomini segnalati.' Vol. II, p. 20.

Napoleon was educated at a royal school, that is to say, at a place where a sophisticated education, usually given by priests, was always fifty years behind the times. Had he been brought up in an establishment remote from Government influence, he might, perhaps, have read Hume and Montesquieu. He might have grasped the strength which public opinion confers upon a Government.

Napoleon gained admission to the École Militaire. In the newspapers of the period may be read an account of how, during one of the first balloon ascents to be made by Blanchard from the Champ de Mars, a young man from the École Militaire tried to force the barriers and did everything possible to climb into the basket; that young man was Bonaparte.

Until now, few anecdotes on this period of his life have been collected. When Turenne was being discussed, a lady remarked: 'I would have preferred it if he had not burned the Palatinate.'

'What matter,' Napoleon replied quickly, 'if the fire were necessary to his plan?'

Napoleon was only fourteen years old at the time.

In 1785 he sat for his entrance examination to the artillery. Out of thirty-six officer vacancies he was twelfth and he was then gazetted to the Régiment de La Fère, as a second lieutenant. In his report, in the section reserved for professors' remarks, beside his name may be read:

'Corsican by character and by nationality, this young man will go far should circumstances prove favourable to him.'

That same year Napoleon lost his father, who died at Montpellier. This misfortune was to some extent palliated by the extreme fondness shown him by his great-uncle Lucien Bonaparte, Archdeacon of Ajaccio. This venerable old man combined rare goodness with a great understanding of mankind. It is said that he discovered the extraordinary talents of his great-nephew, and that he early predicted his future greatness.

It appears that, during the first years which Napoleon spent in the service, he divided his time between his duties as a lieutenant and frequent visits to his family. He wrote a history of Corsica and sent it to Abbé Raynal at Marseilles. The famous historian approved of the young officer's book, advised him to have it printed, and said that it was a work that would endure. It was also added that Napoleon wrote his book in the form of a memorandum to the Government. This memorandum was presented and has doubtless been lost for ever (1790).

The Revolution began. Saint-Cyr was destroyed. Napoleon went to fetch his sister and escort her back to Corsica. As they were walking along the quay at Toulon, they were on the point of being thrown into the sea by the mob which pursued them with cries of 'down with the aristos! down with the black cockade!' Realizing that it was the black ribbon on his sister's hat that these worthy patriots had mistaken for a black cockade, Napoleon stopped, removed the offending ribbon and threw it over the parapet.

In 1791 he was gazetted second Captain to the 4th Artillery Regiment. During the winter of that same year he returned to Corsica and there formed a regiment of volunteers, whose command he was allowed to assume without forfeiting his rank of captain. He had occasion to show coolness and courage during a brawl which arose between his regiment and the National Guard of Ajaccio. Several men were killed and there was much disorder in the town. France declared war on the King of Sardinia. The youthful captain gave the first indication of his military daring by occupying the small islands which lie between Corsica and Sardinia.

[2]

NAPOLEON BECAME AN INTIMATE FRIEND OF BOTH THE famous Paoli and of Pozzo di Borgo, a young Corsican full of ability and ambition. They later became mortal enemies. Friends of Napoleon claim that, from the orders which he heard Paoli give, he guessed that the old general intended to rebel against France. Napoleon ventured to oppose this plan so boldly that ultimately he was imprisoned. He escaped and fled to the mountains, but there he fell into the hands of a band of peasants belonging to the opposing faction. They brought him back to Pozzo di Borgo, who decided to get rid of such a dangerous rival by handing him over to the English. The order, which could have thrown Bonaparte into prison for part of his youth, did not take effect, because the peasants guarding him, either from pity or because they had been won over by him, allowed him to escape.

This second flight took place the night before the day on which he was to have been taken on board an English vessel cruising off the coast. This time he succeeded in reaching the town of Calvi. There he found two French commissioners to whom he revealed the plans of Paoli and of Pozzo di Borgo. Soon afterwards he left Corsica and rejoined the Army of Nice, to which his regiment belonged.

[3]

NAPOLEON WAS PUT IN CHARGE OF SUPERVISING THE batteries between San Remo and Nice. Soon after he was sent on a mission to Marseilles and neighbouring towns. He procured various kinds of munitions for the Army. He was sent on a similar mission to Auxonne, La Fère and Paris. While travelling through the south of France, he encountered civil war between the departments and the Convention (1793). It appeared difficult to obtain from the towns in open revolt against the Government, the ammunition required by the army of that same government. Napoleon succeeded, however, in attaining his object, at times by calling upon the patriotism of the insurgents, at others by taking advantage of their fears. At Avignon, some of the Federalists tried to get him to join them. He replied that he would never fight a civil war. While his mission kept him in the town he had ample opportunity of observing the total incapacity of the generals of both parties, whether royalist or republican. It is common knowledge that Avignon surrendered to Carteaux, who having been a bad painter became a worse general. The young captain wrote a pamphlet ridiculing the story of this siege. He called it: *The Avignon Lunch of Three Soldiers*, 1793.[1]

Upon his return to the Army of Italy from Paris, Napoleon was employed at the siege of Toulon. He found the besieging army still under the orders of Carteaux, an absurd general, jealous of everyone and as incompetent as he was obstinate.

The arrival of Dugommier with reinforcements altered the aspect of the siege. In a letter this clever general of the Convention praised Citizen Bonaparte,[2] Artillery Major, for his conduct during the incident in which General O'Hara was taken prisoner.

Toulon was taken and Bonaparte was promoted to the rank of major. Shortly afterwards he was showing his brother Louis the results of the siege, and pointed out to him a spot where a clumsy attack by Carteaux had caused losses to the Army of the Republic as great as they had been unnecessary. The earth was still ploughed up by cannon-balls. The number of freshly made earthen mounds bore witness to the number of corpses buried there. The ground was littered with the remains of hats, uniforms and arms, which made it almost impossible to walk.

'Look, young man,' said Napoleon to his brother, 'let this be a lesson to you that for a soldier it is as much a matter of conscience as of wisdom to study one's profession seriously. If the wretch who sent those brave men in to attack had known his job,[3] a great many of them would still be alive and serving the Republic. His ignorance sent them to their deaths; they and hundreds like them, in the flower of their youth and at the very moment when they were about to achieve fame and happiness.'

He said this with much feeling and almost with tears in his eyes. It is strange that a man naturally possessed of such lively

[1] Subsequently known as: *Le Souper de Beaucaire*, printed at Avignon in 1793 (Ed. note to French edition.)
[2] *Moniteur* of December 7th, 1793. This is the first time Bonaparte was mentioned in the *Moniteur* where the name was printed: the Citizen Bona-parte.
[3] Perhaps: his business.

feelings of humanity, could, in the years to come, have acquired the soul of a conqueror.

Bonaparte was a major, and commandant of the artillery of the Army of Italy. It was with this rank that he made the siege of Oneglia (1794). He proposed a plan for the invasion of Italy to the commander-in-chief, General Dugommier. Fate was to reserve for him the carrying out of this plan.

He became a brigadier-general, but soon afterwards, as his manners and ability had offended all the generals of the Army, they wrote to Paris and had him appointed to a command in the Vendée. Napoleon abhorred civil war, in which there always seems an inhuman energy. He went post-haste to Paris. There he found that not only had he been transferred from one army to another, but that he had also been transferred from the Artillery to the Line Infantry. Aubry, president of the Military Committee, refused to listen to his protests. He was even refused permission to go out East. He remained in Paris for several months, penniless and unemployed. It was at this period that he became intimate with Talma, the famous actor, also at the start of his career, who gave him theatre tickets whenever he could obtain them.

Napoleon was in the depths of misfortune. He was pulled out of this state of hopeless lethargy, in itself an insult to his character, by Barras who had realized his worth at the siege of Toulon. He put him in command of the troops which were to protect the Convention against Paris. The measures taken by the young general gave the Convention an easy victory. He sought to frighten the citizens of Paris and by doing so avoided killing them. (October 5th, 1795, 13th Vendémiaire.) This important service was rewarded by the post of general, second-in-command of the Army of the Interior.[1]

At the home of Barras, Napoleon met Madame de Beauharnais. She expressed admiration for his conduct; he fell madly in love with her. She was one of the most agreeable people in Paris; and few people have possessed more charm, while Napoleon was

[1] See Barras' report to the Convention in the *Moniteur*.

unspoiled by success with women. He married Josephine (1796) and soon afterwards, at the beginning of spring, Barras and Carnot had him appointed commander-in-chief of the Army of Italy.

[4]

IT WOULD TAKE TOO LONG TO FOLLOW GENERAL BONAPARTE to the battlefields of Montenotte, Arcole and Rivoli. Those immortal victories need to be re-told with all the detail which reveals to the full their miraculous quality.[1] Those victories of a young Republic over an ancient despotism were a great and wonderful era for Europe. For Bonaparte it was the most unsullied and brilliant period of his life. In the course of one year, with a miserable little army which lacked everything, he chased the Germans back from the shores of the Mediterranean to the depths of Carinthia. He scattered and wiped out the ceaselessly renewed armies the House of Austria poured into Italy, and brought peace to the Continent. No general of either ancient or modern times has won so many great battles in so short a space of time, with such inadequate means and over such powerful enemies.[2]

In the course of a single year a young man of twenty-six finds himself in the position of having surpassed an Alexander, a Caesar, a Hannibal and a Frederick. And, as though to console mankind for these blood-stained successes, to the laurels of Mars he joined the olive leaves of civilization. Lombardy had been debased and weakened by centuries of catholicism and despotism,[3] and was little more than a battlefield upon which the Germans came to fight the French. General Bonaparte restored

[1] In expectation of better things, see *Histoire de la guerre*, by General Dumas. *Histoire des campagnes d'Italie*, by General Servan, and above all the *Moniteur* and the *Annual Register*.
[2] See Livy, Book IX, p. 242 (trans. by Dureau de La Malle, Vol. IV, ed. Michaud, 1810).
[3] See the 'how' of this, in Vol. XVI of M. de Sismondi, p. 414.

this most beautiful part of the Roman Empire to life, and in a trice appeared to have also restored its ancient virtues. He turned Lombardy into France's most devoted ally. He made it a republic, and through the institutions which his youthful hands sought to give to it, at the same time accomplished something that was of the greatest use to France and the well-being of the rest of the world.[1]

He behaved, upon every occasion, like a warm and sincere friend to Peace. He deserved the praise, never accorded him, of being the first outstanding figure of the French Republic to set limits upon the aggrandizement of France, and sought sincerely to restore peace to the world. This was doubtless a mistake. But it sprang from a heart that was too trusting and too tender towards the interests of humanity, and was the cause of his greatest mistakes. Posterity, which will clearly see the truth of this, for the honour of the human species, will not wish to believe that the envy of his contemporaries could have transformed this great man into an inhuman monster.[2]

The new French Republic was unable to exist unless surrounded by other republics. The indulgence which General Bonaparte displayed towards the Pope when, with Rome utterly at his mercy, he contented himself with the Treaty of Tolentino and the surrender of a hundred paintings and several statues, made him many enemies in Paris. Nine years later he was forced to carry out dangerously what he could then have accomplished with six thousand men. The Duke of Lodi (Melzi), vice-president of the Italian Republic and a man of integrity with a genuine love of liberty, said that Napoleon concluded the peace of Campo-Formio in direct opposition to the secret orders of the Directory. It was chimerical to believe in any lasting peace between the new Republic and the old European aristocracies.[3]

[1] This ending is rather flat.
[2] See all English books, even the best, between 1800 and 1810 and what is even less generous, the *Considérations* of Mme de Staël written after the massacres at Nîmes.
[3] Stendhal had written first of all: 'the old European dynasties'. He then altered dynasties to aristocracies, adding as a footnote 'dynasties, truer but less clear'. (Ed. note.)

15

[5]

Is it worth taking the trouble to relate the objections raised by people who think they are sensitive when they are merely being weak? Such people claim that the tone used by Bonaparte when offering the Italians their freedom was that of Mahomet reciting the Koran, sword in hand. The converted were praised, protected and loaded with privileges. The infidels were pitilessly delivered up to looting, military executions and all the horrors of war. This amounted to reproaching Napoleon with having used powder to fire his guns. They held the destruction of Venice against him. He did not destroy a republic, but an iniquitous and debased form of government; a weakly led aristocracy, just as the other European governments were strongly led aristocracies. This likeable nation was shocked out of its habitual ways, but the next generation would have been a thousand times happier under a Kingdom of Italy. It is very probable that the transfer of the Venetian States to the House of Austria was one of the secret clauses in the preliminary peace negotiations at Leoben, and that subsequently the reasons alleged for making war on the Republic were no more than pretexts. General Bonaparte started negotiations with men who were discontented so as to be able to occupy the city without firing a shot. In his eyes, it was to the advantage of France to be at peace with Austria. He was the master of Venice, since it was he who had taken it, but it was not his business to see that Venice was happy. One's own country first. In the whole affair there is only one thing with which General Bonaparte may be reproached, and that is that he did not look at things from such an exalted standpoint as the Directory.[1]

[1] To see Napoleon in Italy in a true light, one should steep oneself in a volume of Livy. In that way the mind is cleansed of all the petty, false modern ideas.

[6]

NAPOLEON HAS BEEN REPROACHED WITH CORRUPTING NOT the discipline, but the moral character of his army during his Italian campaign. He encouraged the most scandalous looting among his generals.[1] Forgetting the disinterestedness of the armies of the Republic, they were soon as rapacious as the Commissioners of the Convention. Madame Bonaparte made frequent trips to Genoa, and is said to have put five or six millions safely aside. In this matter Bonaparte behaved criminally towards France. As for Italy, even had the looting been a hundred times worse, it would nevertheless not have been an excessive price to pay for the immense benefit derived from the re-birth of all the national virtues. The crimes to which a revolution gives rise is one of the arguments of the aristocracy. But the crimes which were silently perpetrated before the Revolution are forgotten.

The Army of Italy provided the first examples of soldiers taking a hand in the Government. Until then the Armies of the Republic had been content to defeat their enemies. It is known that in 1797 a party in opposition to the Directory was formed within the Council of the Five Hundred.[2] The plans of the ringleaders may have been innocent, but their conduct certainly laid them open to suspicion. Some of them were undoubted royalists, while the majority very probably had no other thought than to put an end to an arbitrary form of government and to the scandalous corruption of the Directory. The means they adopted were to withdraw the use of taxes from the Government and subject its expenditure to a severe inquiry. Taking advantage of this plan of attack, the Directory spread the rumour throughout the

---

[1] The fortunes of Masséna, Augereau, etc. etc. A major passed through Bologna on his way to an expedition in the Apennines. He didn't even possess a horse. Two weeks later he returned the same way and he had seventeen loaded carts belonging to him, as well as three carriages and two mistresses. Three-quarters of the looted wealth was spent in the country.

[2] Memoirs of Carnot.

armies that all the privations which the men were experiencing were the result of the treachery of the Legislative Body which sought to destroy the country's defenders, so as later to be able to bring back the Bourbons with ease. In a proclamation to his troops, the commander-in-chief of the Army of Italy publicly encouraged these rumours. This Army dared to petition the Government. It allowed itself to make reproaches as violent as they were unconstitutional against the majority of the Legislative Body. Bonaparte's secret intention was to follow up these addresses and to march on Paris with part of his army, under pretext of defending the Directory and the Republic, but in actual fact, to arrogate to himself a leading part in the Government. His plans were upset by the Revolution of 18th Fructidor which took place much sooner and much more easily than he had thought. (September 4th, 1797—18 Fructidor of the Year V.)

This day, which completely wiped out the party in opposition to the Directory, deprived him of any pretext for crossing the Alps. He continued to speak of members of the Directory with the greatest contempt. The negligence, corruption and glaring blunders of the Government were habitual subjects of his conversation. He usually ended by pointing out to the generals around him that, if a man could succeed in conciliating the new way of life inside France with a military form of government, he could easily make the Republic play the part of ancient Rome.

⌈ 7 ⌉

ALTHOUGH NAPOLEON AT ELBA SAID THAT UNTIL HIS CAMpaign in Egypt he continued to be a good Republican, several anecdotes told by Count de Merveldt prove that, at the time of which we are speaking, his republicanism was already very shaky. Merveldt was one of the Austrian negotiators at Leoben and later at Campo-Formio. Since his main interest lay in provoking the downfall of the Republic, he allowed it to be under-

18

stood that General Bonaparte was in a position to take over the leadership of either France or Italy. The General made no reply, but did not appear to be at all shocked at the idea. He even spoke of the experiment of trying to govern France by means of representative bodies and republican institutions as though it were a pure experiment. Encouraged by these inclinations, with the approval of his Court, Merveldt tried proposing a German Principality to Napoleon. The General replied that he was flattered by the offer, which could only arise out of the high opinion they were pleased to have of his ability and of his importance, but that it would hardly be wise, on his part, for him to accept it. Such an establishment would be bound to collapse at the first Austrian war against France, and if France were to win she would proscribe a treacherous citizen who had accepted foreign help. He added frankly that his aim was to obtain a post in the government of his country, and that if ever he could get his foot in the stirrup he had no doubts but that he would go far.

⌈8⌉

HAD NAPOLEON NOT CONCLUDED THE PEACE OF CAMPO-Formio he might have destroyed Austria and spared France the conquests of 1805 and 1809.[1] At this time it appears that this great man was no more than an enterprising soldier possessed of a prodigious genius, but devoid of any fixed political principle. Fired by a thousand ambitions, he had no concrete plan for realizing his ambition.

'It was impossible', said M. Merveldt, 'to have ten minutes' conversation with him without realizing that he was a man of great vision and astounding ability.'

'His speech, ideas and manners', said Melzi, 'were all striking and original. In conversation, as in war, he was brilliant, resourceful, quick to notice and swift to attack his opponent's

[1] Careful.

19

weakness. Gifted with an amazing rapidity of conception, he owed few of his ideas to books, and with the exception of mathematics, he knew little of the sciences. Of all his qualities,' went on Melzi, 'the most remarkable was the astounding ease with which he could concentrate his attention at will upon a given subject, keep it there for several hours in succession without relaxing his attention and as though chained to the subject until he had discovered the best thing to be done in the circumstances. His projects were vast, gigantic, conceived with genius though at times impracticable. They were frequently abandoned in a temper, or rendered impracticable through his own lack of patience. Naturally quick-tempered, decisive, impetuous and violent, he had the amazing gift of being able to make himself charming and, by means of cleverly expressed deference and playful flattery, win over whom he wished. Although usually secretive and reserved, occasionally in a fit of rage or through pride, he would reveal plans it was in his own interest to keep secret. It is very probable that a feeling of affection never made him open his heart.[1]' Anyway the only person he ever loved was Josephine, who never betrayed him. I do not agree that he owed only a few of his ideas to books. He possessed few literary ideas, and it was that which misled the Duke of Lodi, a man of great literary learning who was, in consequence, somewhat weak.

The shot that kills me will bear my name, was one of Napoleon's current expressions. I must admit that I don't understand it. All I find in it is a preliminary tinge of that fatalism natural to men who live in daily peril from gunfire or the sea.

This very great spirit inhabited a pale, thin, almost puny body. The man's activity, the strength with which, despite such a poor physique, he withstood fatigue appeared to his army to be beyond the bounds of possibility. It was one of the main reasons for the incredible enthusiasm which he inspired in the rank and file.[2]

[1] Confused, muddled, to be re-cast.
[2] In the portfolio R. 292 at the Grenoble Library may be found this curious note on the *portraits* of Napoleon Bonaparte:

[9]

SUCH WAS BONAPARTE THE COMMANDER-IN-CHIEF UPON his return to France after the conquest of Italy. He was also the object of French enthusiasm, of the admiration of Europe and of the jealousy of the Government he had served. He was received by this mistrustful Government with every show of confidence and consideration and appointed, even before he reached Paris, one of the plenipotentiary Commissionaires to the Congress assembled at Rastadt for the purpose of making a general peace. Bonaparte lost no time in getting rid of so unsuitable a rôle. The Directory, realizing it was at the head of a young and virile Republic surrounded by enemies who though weakened still remained unreconciled, was too wise to desire peace. Napoleon also refused the command of the Army of England to which he had been appointed. The Directory was not strong enough to carry out such an undertaking successfully. Meanwhile, the young general perceived, what everyone else had also realized, that there was no suitable position for him in France. Even his private life was fraught with danger; his reputation, his whole way of life being rather too romantic and too inspiring. This period of history speaks highly for the integrity of members of the Directory and shows how far we have travelled since the days of Marie de Medicis.

Often at this time and during other moments of discouragement, Bonaparte would long passionately for the calm of private life. He believed he might find happiness in the country.[1]

[1] Here take two pages from Mme la baronne (de Staël).

'Almost all I have seen of him are caricatures. Many painters have given him the inspired eyes of a poet. Such eyes do not go with the astounding capacity for concentration characteristic of his genius. It seems to me that such eyes are expressive of a man who has just allowed his mind to wander or of a man who has just had a sublime vision. His face was beautiful, sometimes exalted, but that was because it was calm. His eyes alone were very vivacious and alert. He smiled frequently, but never laughed. I only once saw him beside himself with joy. That was after hearing Crescentini sing the aria: *Ombra adorata aspetta*. The least bad portraits are those by Robert Lefèvre and Chaudet. The worst those by David and Canova.'

21

[10]

In 1796 he had been sent a plan for the invasion of Egypt. He studied it and returned it to the Directory with his opinion. In mortal perplexity the Directory, remembering this plan, suggested that Napoleon should command the expedition. To have refused an offer of the executive authority for a third time would have led them to believe that some plot was being hatched in France, and it might possibly have caused his downfall. Moreover, the conquest of Egypt was enough to dazzle a superior mind full of imaginative plans and passionately devoted to extraordinary undertakings.

'To think that from the top of those pyramids thirty centuries gaze down upon us', Napoleon said to his army some months later.

Like all European wars, this aggression had only the slightest justification. The French were at peace with the Sultan of Turkey who was the nominal ruler of Egypt, while the Beys, the real masters of the country, were barbarians who, knowing nothing of the law of nations, could hardly offend against it. Besides, such considerations were unlikely to influence greatly the decisions of the young general who probably considered himself to be the country's benefactor in bringing it civilization. The expedition sailed, and by a measure of good fortune which should give food for thought, he was able to reach Alexandria, after taking Malta, without encountering Nelson.

[11]

One must not expect to find here a detailed account of that series of major military engagements which placed Egypt under the rule of Bonaparte. To understand the battles of Cairo, the Pyramids and Aboukir, a description of Egypt is needed, and some idea should be given of the sublime courage of the Mamelukes. The main difficulty lay in teaching our troops to resist them.[1]

Napoleon made war in Egypt upon the same principles as in Italy, but in a more despotic and Oriental manner. Moreover, he was confronted by the most arrogant and ferocious of men, by a people who only lacked aristocracy to be Romans. He punished their perfidy with a cruelty which he borrowed from them. The people of Cairo rose against the garrison. Not content with making an example of those caught carrying arms, he suspected their priests of being the secret instigators of the rising and he had two hundred of them taken out and shot.

Bourgeois historians gloss over such incidents with empty phrases. The semi-intelligent justify them by the cruelty and brutality of the Turks who, not content with massacring hospital patients and some prisoners they had taken, in circumstances too revolting to be described, ruthlessly mutilated their corpses in the most savage manner as well.

One must seek the reason for these unfortunate though necessary measures in the consequences which result from applying the principle of: *Salus populi suprema lex esto.*[2] A despotism beyond the reach of calumny has so debased the Oriental, that they know no other rule of obedience than fear.[3] The Cairo massacre filled them with terror, 'and since that time', Napoleon was wont to say, 'they have been much attached to me, for they saw that there was no softness in the way I governed'.

[1] See the description of Egypt in Volney's *Histoire militaire.* Also the weak Martin, Berthier, Denon, Wilson at that time quite worthy to be one of the authoritative writers.
[2] Sic.
[3] See the *Liège Commentary* for the correction of this sentence. December 14th, 1817.*

*M. Royer points out that Stendhal means to refer here to the *Commentaire sur l'Esprit des Lois* by Destutt de Tracy. Liège, 1817.

[12]

THE MIXTURE OF CATHOLICISM AND ARISTOCRACY WHICH
has ironed out our souls for the past two hundred years, blinds
us to the consequences of the principle to which I have just
referred. Without entering into the petty reproaches made to
Napoleon on the subject of his conduct in Egypt, his greatest
crimes are generally considered to have been:

1. The killing of his prisoners at Jaffa.
2. The poisoning of his sick at Acre.
3. His feigned conversion to Mohammedanism.
4. His desertion of the army.

Napoleon gave the following account of the Jaffa incident to
Lord Ebrington, one of the most enlightened and reliable of all
the travellers whom Napoleon saw at Elba.

'As for the Turks at Jaffa, it is true that I had about two
thousand of them shot.[1] You feel that that was going too far?
But I had let them surrender at El Arish on condition that they
returned to Baghdad. They violated the terms of this capitulation and rushed into Jaffa where I then took them by storm. I
was unable to take them with me as prisoners, because I was
short of bread and they were devils too dangerous to be released
in the desert a second time. Therefore, there was nothing else
I could do but kill them.'

According to the rules of war it is true that a prisoner who
has once broken parole has no further right to mercy.[2] But the
appalling rights of a conqueror have seldom been exercised and
never, it seems to me, in modern times upon so great a number of
men at once. If, in the heat of the attack, the French had refused
to give any quarter, no one would have blamed them, since the
men killed had broken parole. If the victorious general had
realized that a considerable number of the garrison consisted of

[1] See Las Cases.
[2] See Martens: *Lois des Nations*, p. 291.

24

prisoners sent back to El Arish on parole, he would probably have given orders for them to be put to the sword. I do not think there is another example in history of a garrison spared at the time of assault, being subsequently put to death. But that is not all. It is probable that not more than a third of the Jaffa garrison consisted of prisoners from El Arish.[1]

In order to save his army, has a general the right to kill his prisoners or to place them in a position which will inevitably cause their death or hand them over to savages from whom they can expect no quarter? With the Romans there would have been no question about it.[2] Furthermore, upon the answer to this question depends not only the justification of Napoleon at Jaffa, but of Henry V at Agincourt, of Lord Anson in the South Sea Islands and of the Bailli de Suffren on the coast of Coromandel. One thing is certain, and that is that the need must be obvious and imperative. It cannot be denied that the need existed in the case of the Jaffa incident. It would have been unwise to have sent the prisoners back on parole. Experience had shown that these savages would have had no scruples about setting themselves up in the first fortified town they encountered; or that attaching themselves to the army as it advanced into Palestine, they would constantly have harried its flanks and rear-guard.

The commander-in-chief should not alone be held responsible for this appalling action. The decision was taken at a Council of War at which Berthier, Kléber, Lannes, Bon, Caffarelli and several other generals were present.

[13]

NAPOLEON HAS HIMSELF TOLD SEVERAL PEOPLE THAT HE intended having opium administered as a poison to some of the sick of his army. It is obvious to anyone who knew him that this

---

[1] See Las Cases.
[2] See Livy who reproaches the Samnites with reason for not having wiped out the Romans at the Caudine Forks. Book IX.

idea was the result of an error of judgement, and was not at all due to callousness and even less to indifference to the fate of his soldiers. All accounts[1] agree as to the care he took of the sick and wounded during the Syrian campaign. He did something no general had ever done before; he personally visited the hospitals for the plague-stricken. He talked to the patients, listened to their complaints and saw for himself that the surgeons were carrying out their duties.[2]

Every time his army moved and especially during the retreat from Acre, his greatest care was for his hospital. The wisdom of the measures taken to transport the sick and wounded and the care given them, won the praise of the English. M. Desgenettes, who was chief medical officer to the Army of Syria, is nowadays a pronounced royalist, but even since the return of the Bourbons he has never spoken of Napoleon's conduct towards his sick except in terms of the highest praise.

The celebrated Assalini, a doctor at Munich, was also in Syria at the time and although he disliked Napoleon, he speaks of him as did Desgenettes. At the time of the retreat from Acre, Assalini having made a report to the chief medical officer from which it transpired that the means of transport for the sick were inadequate, he received instructions to go out upon the roads and to stop all baggage animals and even to take the officers' horses. This drastic measure was fully carried out, and not one of the sick was left behind who, in the opinion of the doctors, stood the slightest chance of recovery. At Elba, the Emperor, who felt that the English nation counted among its citizens the sanest heads in Europe, invited Lord Ebrington on several occasions to question him frankly on incidents in his life. As a result of this permission, when Lord Ebrington came to the rumours of poisoning, Napoleon replied immediately and without the slightest hesitation:

'There is a modicum of truth in it. Several soldiers had the

---

[1] Even the slanderous account by General Robert Wilson.
[2] He tried to persuade M. Desgenettes to maintain in public that the plague was not contagious. The vanity of the latter caused him to refuse.

26

plague. They could not have lived more than twenty-four hours. I was on the point of leaving. I consulted Desgenettes as to the means of taking them with us. He replied that we would run the risk of infecting the whole army with the plague, and that moreover such care would be wasted on the patients, as they could not recover. I told him to give them a dose of opium, since that would be better than leaving them to the mercy of the Turks.[1] Like a man of honour he replied that it was his business to cure and not to kill. Possibly he was right, although I only asked him to do for them what I would have asked my best friends to do for me under similar circumstances. I have often pondered the ethics of this since, and I have asked several people for their opinion. *I believe that fundamentally it is always better to let a man fulfil his destiny no matter what it may be.* I came to this conclusion later, at the death of my poor friend Duroc who, with his guts spilling to the ground before me, begged me several times and even pleaded that I should put an end to his sufferings. I told him: 'I pity you, my friend, but there is nothing to be done, you must endure to the end.'

As for Napoleon's apostasy in Egypt, he began all his proclamations with the words: '*Allah is Allah and Mohammed is his prophet.*' This alleged crime created no effect anywhere except in England. Other nations realized that it should be put in the same category as the Mohammedanism of Major Horneman and the other travellers whom the Africa Society employed to discover the secrets of the desert. Napoleon wished to conciliate the Egyptians.[2] He was right in hoping that a large section of this congenitally superstitious people would be struck with terror at his religious and prophetic sentences and that they would even surround his person with an aura of irresistible fatalism. The idea that he seriously desired to be taken for a second Mohammed, is worthy of an *émigré*.[3] His conduct met with the most unqualified success.

[1] See Las Cases.
[2] See the article by Las Cases.
[3] See their books.

'You can have no idea', he told Lord Ebrington, 'of what I gained in Egypt through pretending to adopt their religion.'

The English, for ever dominated by their Puritan prejudices which nevertheless go hand-in-glove with the most revolting cruelties, thought that this was a low trick. History will show that towards the time of Napoleon's birth, Catholic ideas were already subject to ridicule.

[14]

AS FOR THE MUCH MORE SERIOUS ACT OF ABANDONING HIS army in Egypt, that was primarily a crime against the Government which it could legitimately punish. But it was not a crime against his army, which he left in a flourishing condition, as is proved by the way in which it withstood the English. The only thing he may be reproached with is the blunder of not having foreseen that Kléber might be killed, which subsequently committed the army to the ineptitude of General Menou.

We shall know in time whether, as I believe, Napoleon was recalled to France on the advice of several clever patriots or whether he determined upon this decisive step solely as a result of his own reflections.[1] The compassionate will take pleasure in wondering what must have taken place in his mind at that time. On the one hand there was ambition and love of country; the hope of leaving a great name to posterity, while on the other there was the possibility of being captured by the English or of being shot.[2] What firmness of judgement to take such a decisive course based solely upon conjecture! This man's whole life is a paean in praise of greatness of soul.

[1] This is a very interesting question that one should try to clarify in a work such as this. (Note by Vismara.)

Nothing can be done before the publication of the Mémoires of Lucien, Sieyès and Barras. (Note by Stendhal.)

[2] Something should be said of the way in which he left the army and of his departure, which was an event bordering on the grandiose. (Note by Vismara.)

Yes, I will do so. (Note by Stendhal.)

[15]

WHEN NAPOLEON HEARD OF THE LOSS OF ITALY, THE disasters to the armies and the anarchy and discontent inside the country, he concluded from this sorry picture that the Directory could no longer survive. He returned to Paris so as to save France and to make certain of a place for himself in the new Government. By his return from Egypt he served both the country and himself; which is all that can be asked of mere mortals.[1]

To be sure, after he had landed, Napoleon had no idea of how he would be treated. Until his enthusiastic reception at Lyons, it looked doubtful whether his daring would be rewarded by a throne or the scaffold. At the first news of his return, the Directory instructed Fouché, then Minister of Police, to arrest him. This famous traitor replied: 'He is not the man to let himself be arrested; nor am I the man to arrest him.'[2]

[16]

WHILE GENERAL BONAPARTE WAS HASTENING BACK FROM Egypt to the help of the country, Barras, a member of the Directory and an excellent man for an underhand deal, was engaged in selling France to the exiled royal family for the sum of twelve million francs. With this aim in view, letters patent had already been sent. Barras had been pursuing the matter for two

[1] Details of the sea-trip.
[2] Every day new* . . . were to be found at the gates of the Luxemburg. For instance, one day a large poster was to be seen representing a lancet, a lettuce and a rat. This was a play on the words lancette laitre rat (*L'an sept les tuera*. The seventh year will kill them.)

*Blank in the text.

29

years, and Sieyès had discovered the plot while ambassador at Berlin.[1] This example with that of Mirabeau shows clearly that a republic should never entrust itself to men of noble birth. Having always been susceptible to the charm of an official title, Barras dared to confide his plans to his former protégé.

Napoleon had found his brother Lucien in Paris and together they discussed the following possibilities. It was obvious that either he or the Bourbons were going to ascend the throne, or the Republic would have to be remodelled.

The plan to restore the Bourbons was absurd. The people still loathed the nobility and, despite the crimes of the Terror, they were still devoted to the Republic. The Bourbons would need a foreign army inside Paris. As for remodelling the Republic, Napoleon did not feel that he had at his disposal the means of resolving the problem and of giving France a constitution that would endure. He had found the available men too despicable and devoted solely to their own interests. Finally, he could see no assured position for himself, and if there should happen to be another traitor ready to sell France to the Bourbons or to England, his death was the first thing to be accomplished. As was only natural in this state of uncertainty, ambition carried the day and in self-justification Napoleon told himself: 'I am better for France than the Bourbons.' As for the constitutional monarchy desired by Sieyès, he had no means of establishing it and also the king he proposed was too little known. An energetic and immediate remedy was needed.

Unfortunate France, internally chaotic, witnessed the collapse of all her armies, one after the other. Her enemies were kings whose duty it was to show her no mercy, since the Republic, by showing their peoples the way to happiness, imperilled their thrones. If after defeating France these exasperate kings had condescended to restore the country to the exiled royal family,

[1] Barras' intermediaries were MM. David, Mounier, Tropès de Guérin, the Duke de Fleury. See the *Biographie Moderne* by Michaud for an invaluable effusion on the subject as a result of such admissions. The *Moniteur* paints a good picture of the chaos and the degradation.

what that family was later to do or to permit in 1815[1] still gives only a feeble idea of what in 1800[2] might have been expected of it. Sunk to the utmost depth of discouragement and moral degradation, unfortunate in the government she herself had so proudly chosen, even more unfortunate in the rout of her armies, France would not have inspired the Bourbons with any fear. And the liberal aspect of the government can be attributed solely to the people's fear of a king.

It is highly probable that the victorious kings would have divided France among themselves. It would have been wise to destroy such a hot-bed of Jacobinism. The Duke of Brunswick's manifesto could then have been carried out and all those fine writers who adorn the Academies could have proclaimed liberty to be an impossibility. Since 1793, new ideas had never been in greater peril. World civilization was about to be thrust back several centuries. The unhappy Peruvian would still have groaned under the iron yoke of the Spaniard, and the victorious kings would have given themselves to the refinements of cruelty, as at Naples.[3]

Therefore, on all sides France was about to vanish into the bottomless abyss in which in our times we have seen Poland engulfed.

If ever circumstances existed which were capable of laying down the eternal right of all mankind to a boundless freedom, General Bonaparte was in a position to say to every Frenchman: 'Through me you are still French. Through me you are not subject to a Prussian judge or a Piedmontese governor. Through me you are not the slave of some irate master seeking to avenge his own fear. Suffer me then to be your Emperor.'

Such were the principal ideas which animated General Bonaparte and his brother on the eve of the 18 Brumaire (November 9th, 1799). Everything else merely related to the means of carrying them out.

[1] The mission of the Marquis de Rivière to the South. The Nîmes massacres. The Trestaillon incident.
[2] Careful. Credit the émigrés with what they did in 1815.
[3] Careful. Delete this sentence.

WHILE NAPOLEON WAS DECIDING UPON HIS COURSE OF
action and the means of putting it into force, he was also being
courted by the different factions which rent the dying Republic.
The Government was about to fall through lack of a conservative Senate able to maintain the balance between the Chamber
of Commons and the Directory, as well as able to appoint
members to the Directory, and not because a republic is impossible in France. In this case a dictator was needed, but the
legitimately established government would never have brought
itself to name one. The sordid spirits who had grown to maturity
under an ancient monarchy, and who now constituted the
Directory, were only aware, in the midst of their country's misfortunes, of their own petty egoisms and interests. Everything
the least bit generous seemed to them nothing more than a
fraud.

The wise and good Sieyès had always clung to the great
principle that to guarantee the institutions gained by the
Revolution, what was needed was a dynasty called into being by
the Revolution. He helped Bonaparte to bring about the 18
Brumaire. Failing him, he would have done it with some other
general. Sieyès has since said: 'I made the 18 Brumaire, but not
the 19.' It has been said that General Moreau refused to support
Sieyès, and that General Joubert, who had aspired to that rôle,
was killed at the beginning of his first battle, at Novi.

Sieyès and Barras were the two chief men in the Government.
Barras sold the Republic to a Bourbon without worrying about
the consequences, and asked General Bonaparte to lead the
movement. Sieyès wished to create a constitutional monarchy.
The first article in his constitution would have named a Duke
of Orleans king, and he asked General Bonaparte to lead the
movement. The General, who was necessary to both parties,
approached Lefèvre, a general better known for his daring than
for his intelligence, and who at the time was in command of Paris

and of the 17th Division. Bonaparte acted in agreement with Barras and Sieyès, but he had soon won General Lefèvre to himself. From that moment Bonaparte controlled the troops occupying Paris and its environs; and the only remaining question was what shape the Revolution was to assume.

[18]

DURING THE NIGHT OF 18 BRUMAIRE (9 NOVEMBER, 1799), Bonaparte suddenly called together by means of personal letters those members of the Council of *Anciens* on whom he could count. Advantage was taken of the article in the Constitution which enabled the Council to transfer the Legislative Body outside Paris. The Council passed a decree which, on the following day, 19 Brumaire, gave notice of a meeting of the Legislative Body at Saint-Cloud; it engaged General Bonaparte to take all precautions necessary for the safety of the national representatives and placed the troops of the Line and the National Guards under his orders. Called to the bar to hear this decree, Bonaparte made a speech. As he could not refer to the two conspiracies he was about to frustrate, his speech consisted only of empty phrases. On the 19th the Directory, the generals and a crowd of sightseers went to Saint-Cloud. Soldiers lined all the streets. The Council of Ancients was assembled in the gallery. The Council of the Five Hundred, of which Lucien Bonaparte had just been made President, met in the Orangerie. Bonaparte entered the Chamber of the *Anciens* and spoke amidst the interruptions and cries of deputies devoted to the Constitution, or perhaps it would be better to say, those who refused to let a movement succeed to which they were not a party. During these critical moments, an even more stormy scene was taking place at the Council of the Five Hundred. Several members demanded that the motives which had determined the removal of the Councils to Saint-Cloud, should be examined. Lucien made fruitless attempts to calm those who had been roused by this proposal, and when the French reach such a pitch, self-interest becomes submerged, or rather, there remains no other course than to become a hero out of vanity. The general cry was: 'No dictator! Down with the dictator!'

At that moment General Bonaparte entered the Chamber escorted by four grenadiers. A crowd of deputies cried:

'What is the meaning of this? No swords in here! No armed men!' Others, better judges of events, rushed into the middle of the council-chamber, surrounded the general, and seizing hold of him roughly shook him and cried: 'Outlaw! Down with the dictator!' As bravery in council-chambers is a very rare thing in France, history would do well to remember the name of Deputy Bigonnet of Mâcon. This brave deputy should have killed Bonaparte.

The rest of the account is less reliable. It is asserted that upon hearing the terrible cry of 'outlaw!' Bonaparte grew pale and could not find a single word to say in self-defence.[1] General Lefèvre came to his assistance and helped him to get away. It is added that Bonaparte jumped upon a horse and believing the coup at Saint-Cloud to have failed, galloped towards Paris. He was still upon the bridge when Murat succeeded in rejoining him and told him that: 'he who leaves a fight, loses it'. Restored to his senses by this saying, Napoleon returned to the rue de Saint-Cloud, called the soldiers to arms and sent a picket of grenadiers into the council-chamber of the Orangerie. These grenadiers, led by Murat, entered the council-chamber. Lucien, who had held out in the tribune, returned to the chair and declared that those representatives who had wished to assassinate his brother were audacious bandits in the pay of England. He had a decree passed suppressing the Directory and placing the executive power in the hands of three provisional Consuls: Bonaparte, Sieyès and Roger-Ducos. A legislative commission, to be

[1] I believe it to be the duty of an historian of his own times, to write only of known facts and not of doubts or of hearsay. This incident must be clarified or else cut. (Note by Vismara.) No. (Note by Stendhal.)

selected from both councils, was to join the three Consuls for the purpose of drawing up a constitution.

Until the publication of the *Mémoires* of Lucien,[1] details of 18 Brumaire will not be very clear. In the meantime, the honours of this great revolution go to the President of the Council of the Five Hundred who displayed in the tribune a dauntless courage at a time when his brother had weakened. He greatly influenced the Constitution that was hastily being drafted. This Constitution which was not bad, appointed three Consuls: Bonaparte, Cambacérès and Lebrun.

A *Senate* was formed, composed of people who could lay claim to no position. This Senate appointed the *Legislative Body* which could vote laws, but could not debate them. This was reserved for another body known as the *Tribunat* which debated laws, but could not vote them.

Both the *Tribunat* and the executive power sent their draft laws to be defended before the silent *Legislative Body*.

This Constitution might have worked quite well, had the fortunes of France willed that the First Consul be removed by a bullet after a reign of two years. The country would then have seen enough of the monarchy to have been completely disgusted with it. It is easy to see that the fault of the Constitution of the Year VIII lay in the fact that the Legislative Body was appointed by the Senate. It should have been elected directly by the people, and the Senate charged with appointing a new Consul every year.

[19]

A GOVERNMENT OF A DOZEN COWARDLY AND TREACHEROUS thieves was replaced by a military despotism. But without this military despotism, France would have had in 1800 the events of 1814, or else the Terror. Napoleon now had his foot in the

---

[1] These *Mémoires* are already with Colburn at London. They may be published at any moment, as well as those of Carnot and of Tallien.

stirrup, as he had remarked during his Italian campaign. And it must be admitted that never has a general or a monarch had so brilliant a year as was the last year of the eighteenth century both for him and for France.

When he assumed power the First Consul found the armies of France defeated and disorganized. His Italian conquests were reduced to the mountains and coast of Genoa. He had just lost the greater part of Switzerland. The greed and injustice of the Republican agents[1] had shocked the Swiss. From then on the aristocracy gained the upper hand in that country, and France had no more inveterate enemy. Their neutrality was but a name, and the most vulnerable French frontier was completely unprotected.

All French resources were completely exhausted and, worst of all, the enthusiasm of the French was dead. All attempts to establish a free constitution had failed. The Jacobins were hated and despised for their cruelty as well as for the folly of having sought to establish a republic modelled on those of antiquity. The moderates were despised for their incapacity and corruption. The Royalists, who were very active in Western France, as usual proved themselves in Paris to be timid, intriguers and above all cowards.[2]

With the exception of Moreau, nobody who had returned from Egypt, other than the General, possessed both popularity and a reputation. And Moreau at that time wished to go with the crowd, which at all times he was incapable of leading.

[20]

WASHINGTON HIMSELF WOULD HAVE FOUND IT DIFFICULT to judge the amount of liberty to be granted safely to a supremely childish people, for whom experience meant nothing

---

[1] Quite by chance the most knavish of these rascals was called Rapinat.

[2] Careful. They were above all unenterprising. *For me* (in English in the text) their finest characteristic. The Lyons conspiracy of 1817.

and who at heart still cherished all the stupid prejudices to which an ancient monarchy gives rise.

But none of the ideas which would have preoccupied Washington held the attention of the First Consul; perhaps he merely considered them too weak and visionary for Europe in the year 1800. General Bonaparte was exceedingly ignorant of the art of government. Bred on military ideas, to him discussion had always seemed insubordination. Experience proved to him daily his immense personal superiority and he despised men too much to let them discuss measures which he had deemed salutary. Imbued with Roman ideas, the greatest misfortune, in his eyes, was to be conquered and not to be badly governed and pestered in one's own home.

Had he possessed a more understanding mind; even if he had understood the invincible power which government by public opinion confers, I have no doubt that the man would have carried the day, and that in the long run the despot would have appeared. It is not given to one human being to have all the talents at once, and he was too superb a general to be any good as a politician and legislator.

During the first months of his consulate, he exercised a veritable dictatorship which events rendered necessary. Hounded internally by the Jacobins and the Royalists and by the memory of the recent conspiracies of Barras and of Sieyès, harassed externally by the armies of the kings ever ready to swarm over the territory of the Republic, the primary law was to survive. In my eyes this law justified all the arbitrary measures he took during the first years of his consulate.

Gradually as their conception of him was borne out by experience, people came to believe that his opinions were entirely original. At once a horde of sycophants surrounded him. As usual they obviously exaggerated all opinions attributed to the Master.[1] Men of the type of Regnault and Maret were assisted by a nation accustomed to slavery and which only feels at ease when being led.

[1]Carrion-Nisas in 1801, or Ferrand in 1815.

It was not Napoleon's aim to give the French people at first as much freedom as they could stand, and then gradually to increase this freedom proportionately as the factious parties cooled down and public opinions grew calmer and more enlightened. He did not consider how much authority could safely be entrusted to the people; he only sought to discover with how little power they would be content. The constitution which he gave to France was calculated, if indeed it were calculated, gradually to bring a fine country back to an absolute monarchy and not to complete the fashioning of it along lines of freedom.[1] Napoleon saw a crown before his eyes and let himself be dazzled by the splendour of that out of date bauble. He might have established the Republic[2] or at least set up a government by two Chambers. But his sole ambition was to found a dynasty of kings.

[21]

THE FIRST MEASURES TAKEN BY THE DICTATOR WERE noble, wise and beneficial. Everyone was agreed on the need for a strong government; so a strong government there was. Everyone protested at the corruption and lack of equity of recent governments; the First Consul put a stop to petty thieving and lent a strong arm to the administration of justice. Everyone deplored the existence of parties which divided and weakened France; Napoleon placed men of ability from all parties at the head of affairs. Everyone feared a reaction; with a firm hand Napoleon suppressed all reactionary attempts. His government also protected all those who obeyed the laws, and ruthlessly

[1] The Consul's actions are as much a part of European history as of French history.

[2] Five Directors to be renewed every five years and who were nominated by a conservative Senate. Two Chambers directly elected by the people, the first from among those paying 1,000 francs in taxes; the second from among those paying 10,000 francs in taxes, to be renewed every five years. Such a government is a sure guarantee against conquest.

punished all who sought to infringe them. Persecution had revived the last sparks of Catholicism; Napoleon took religious worship under his protection and restored the priests to their altars. The western departments were ravaged by a civil war which the law of hostages had caused to flare up again; Napoleon abolished the law of hostages, closed the lists of *émigrés* and, by a judicious mixture of softness and severity he restored complete calm to the west. The whole of France was united in a desire for peace; Napoleon offered to make peace with his enemies. After his offer had been disdainfully rejected by England and by Austria, he subdued the latter power by means of the admirable Marengo campaign, and then pardoned her with extravagant generosity. The English Cabinet, that poisonous oligarchy which employs the strength and knowledge it owes to freedom[1] to increase the misfortunes of the world and to rivet the fetters of the enslaved; the English Cabinet, the most formidable and enlightened of all the First Consul's enemies, deserted by all its allies, was ultimately obliged to make peace and to recognize the Republic.

[22]

NAPOLEON ALREADY HAD NO FURTHER RIVALS AMONG THE great men of modern times.[2] He had reached the pinnacle of fame, and had he wished to give freedom to his country, he would no longer have encountered any obstacle.

Above all he was praised for having restored peace to the Church by means of his Concordat. This was a great mistake which will delay by a century the emancipation of France. He

---

[1] Tedious. Detracts from the main subject. To be inserted elsewhere as well as the English aristocracy's fear of the freedom which existed across the Channel. The English, after having feared our armed forces under Napoleon, are now afraid of our freedom.

[2] (In English in the text.) 'Note of a great man. I would have added some observations and some anecdotes, here and there, but the departure has robbed me of the opportunity.'

should have been satisfied with putting an end to all persecution.[1] Private individuals have to pay their priest as they do their baker.

He always observed the greatest tolerance towards French Protestants. In his time, any man who had spoken of the possible violation of this primary right of man would have been thought mad. Putting his finger upon the sore which hinders the recovery of Catholicism, he asked the Pope to authorize the marriage of priests, but he met with little comprehension at the court of Rome. As he told Fox, if he had insisted on pursuing this objective, *they would have cried that it was pure Protestantism.*

He introduced more fairness and rapidity into the administration of justice. He was busy on the Code Napoléon, his finest work. Thus, as an example unique in history, it is to her greatest military leader that France owes the disappearance of the confusion and contradictions which existed in the intricacies of the laws by which she was governed. Finally crime disappeared, thanks to the appearance of the policemen whom he had chosen from among his finest soldiers.

⌈ 23 ⌉

BUT ON TURNING FROM HIS ADMINISTRATION TO EXAMINE his institutions, the picture changes. On the one hand all is light, happiness and sincerity, while on the other all is uncertainty, pettiness and hypocrisy.

Napoleon's political mistakes may be summed up in a few words. He was always afraid of the masses and he never had a

---

[1] On the contrary once he had taken up a position on the side of a monarchy, Napoleon, who had no new political ideas, was obliged to surround himself with religion, and to lend it distinction, etc. . . . (Note by Vismara.)

He did not need the Concordat to be able to reign over a nation that was extremely indifferent to religion. The only serious obstacle he encountered was the Pope, at Savona. If he had not made the Concordat, the Pope would always have been at his feet. This was admirably expressed to Napoleon by the Third Consul, Lebrun. (Note by Stendhal.)

plan. Nevertheless, guided unwittingly by the natural soundness of his mind and the respect he always felt for the Constituent Assembly, the institutions which he founded were always liberal. To be sure, a silent Legislative Body, a Tribunat that can debate but not vote, a Senate that debates in secret are absurd, because a government cannot represent only half general opinion. 'But, we told ourselves, it takes a Romulus to found States, and then Numa follows.' After his death it was an easy matter to perfect these institutions and make them bring forth liberty. Furthermore, for the French, they had the tremendous advantage of making them forget everything old. Frenchmen need to be cured of their respect for outworn ideas, and had Napoleon been better advised, he would have restored Parliament. In the midst of so many miracles that were the products of his genius, the First Consul saw only an empty throne, and in fairness to him it must be said that neither his military habits nor his temperament were suited to the restrictions imposed by a limited authority. The Press, which had dared, most inconveniently, to bring things to light, was persecuted and subdued. People who incurred his displeasure were threatened, arrested and banished without trial. Personal freedom had no other refuge against the arbitrary orders of his Minister of Police, than the extent of his genius which made him realize that all kinds of useless irritation diminished the strength of the nation and, in consequence, that of its sovereign ruler. So great was the power of this controlling influence that, although he reigned over forty million subjects and followed upon governments which had, as it were, encouraged every crime, the State prisons were less full than under good King Louis XVI. There was a tyrant, but little despotism. Nevertheless, civilization's real cry is: 'No despotism!'

He acted from day to day according to his moods which were terrible, against the political bodies which alone induced fear in that intrepid mind. One fine day, after the Tribunat had dared to produce sound arguments against the projected laws advanced by his ministers, he hunted all elements of any value whatsoever out of the Tribunat and shortly afterwards suppressed it entirely. The Senate, far from being conservative, experienced constant changes and was repeatedly debased because Bonaparte did not want any organization to take root in public opinion. It was essential for an extremely discriminating people to sense in the words *stability* and *posterity* that there was nothing stable except his power, nothing progressive except his authority. 'The French', he remarked at about this time, 'are indifferent to liberty. They neither understand it nor like it. Vanity is their ruling passion and political equality, which enables them to feel that any position is open to them, is the only political right they care about.'

Never has anything more true been said about the French people.[1]

Under the Emperor, political training caused Frenchmen to cry *A la Liberté* more often than they actually felt the need. That is why the suppression of the freedom of the Press was so well calculated. The nation showed itself to be completely indifferent when the First Consul deprived it of freedom of the Press and individual liberty. Today France suffers deeply from their absence. To be fair, in the past she did not feel events with the sensitivity of today. Then the bringing of the sword of Frederick (the victor of Rosbach) to the Invalides, consoled her for the loss of a privilege. Tyrannical measures were frequently used in the common interest. For instance, the merging of the political parties, the financial agreements, the instituting of the Code, and the undertakings of the Department of Communications. It is possible, on the other hand, to imagine a government which causes little or no inconvenience to the individual because it is weak, yet which employs its small amount of strength to the annoyance of general interest.

The First Consul was thoroughly convinced that vanity in France was a national characteristic. To satisfy both his own ambition and this all-pervading passion, he took care to aggran-

[1] *For me.* What proves the stupidity of the Bourbons to me, is that seeking unrestricted pleasure, they have not followed this same path.

dize France and to increase its influence in Europe. When one morning the Parisian read in his *Moniteur* a decree beginning: *Holland has been reunited with the Empire,* he admired the might of France, realized that Napoleon was vastly superior to Louis XIV, and gloried in obeying such a leader, forgot that only the previous day he had been irritated by conscription or indirect taxation, and merely thought of applying for a post in Holland for his son.

At the time of which we are speaking, Piedmont, the Parma States and the Island of Elba successively were annexed to the Republic. These partial reunions were matter for conversation. When Melzi put before Napoleon his fears on the subject of the reunion of Piedmont, the First Consul replied with a smile: 'This is a strong arm; it only asks for loads to carry.' Spain ceded Louisiana to him. He gained possession of Saint-Domingo by means which are not clearly known, yet which would appear to be worthy of the treachery and cruelty of Philip II. He assembled at Lyons all the outstanding figures of that Cisalpine Republic, the one fine creation of his political genius. He deprived them of their dreams of liberty and forced them to make him their president. The Genoese aristocracy, more contemptible than the Venetian, was saved for a time by the shrewdness of one of its nobles who, at first a friend of Napoleon, later underwent several years persecution as a result of that flash of patriotism. Helvetia was forced to accept his mediation. Yet while he prevented the birth of liberty in Italy, he sought to revive it in Switzerland. He brought the Canton of Vaud into existence and saved that beautiful country, where liberty survives even today, from the degrading tyranny of the Bernese aristocracy. Germany was divided and re-divided among its princes according to his ideas, those of Russia and the corruption of its minister.

In the course of a single year, such were the exploits of this great man.

Writers of scurrilous lampoons as well as Madame de Staël, saw only misfortune in this for the human species, while actually it was just the opposite. For the past century it is not good intentions that have been lacking in Europe, but the energy required to shift the massive bulk of established customs. Henceforth, any great movement can only benefit morale which means the happiness of the human race. Every shock to which all such worn-out ideas are subjected, brings them closer to genuine stability.[1]

It is asserted that upon his return from the electoral meeting at Lyons, the First Consul thought of having himself proclaimed Emperor of the Gauls. Ridicule served him well. On the boulevards could be seen a caricature which depicted a child shepherding some turkeys with a long thin pole (*gaule*) and underneath was the caption: *Empire of the Gauls*. The Consular Guard proved by its murmurs that it had not forgotten his cry of: *Long Live the Republic*, which had so often led them to victory. Lannes, the bravest of his generals, who had twice saved his life in Italy, and whose friendship for Napoleon bordered on the passionate, made a scene in his presence, in defence of republicanism.

But a subservient Senate and a heedless people made him Consul for life with power to designate his successor. There remained nothing further for him to desire except an empty title. The extraordinary events which we are about to describe, clothed him soon after in Imperial purple.[2]

[24]

THE FIRST CONSUL'S MODERATION, IN CONTRAST TO THE violence of previous governments, filled the royalists with wild and boundless hopes. The Cromwell of the French Revolution had just appeared, and they were simple-minded enough to see in him a second General Monk. Realizing their mistake, they

---

[1] See those states which were reorganized after Napoleon's downfall. Compare them with what they were before conquest. Geneva, Frankfort . . . etc. A nation's traditions are its wealth.

[2] Perhaps delete: soon after.

sought to avenge their misplaced hopes and it was this that produced the infernal machine.

An unknown man asked a child to look after a small handcart on which was a barrel. This was at night, at the entrance to the rue Saint-Nicaise. Seeing the carriage of the First Consul leaving the Tuileries on its way to the Opera, the unknown man walked quickly away. Instead of stopping before the little cart which was in its way, the Consul's coachman put his horses to the gallop at risk of overturning the cart.[1] Two seconds later the cart exploded with a terrific noise, scattering far and wide the bodies of the unfortunate child and of some thirty people who were in the street at the time. The Consul's carriage was saved although no more than twenty feet from the cart, because it had just turned the corner into the rue de Malte.[2] Napoleon always believed that Lord Wyndham, the English Minister in Paris, had lent a helping hand to this undertaking. He said as much to Fox during the celebrated conversation which these two great men had at the Tuileries. Fox strongly denied it, then fell back upon the well-known integrity of the English Government. Napoleon who had an infinite respect for him, had the good manners not to laugh.[3]

The peace with England which had been concluded in the meantime, put an end to Royalist intrigues, but soon afterwards, when war again broke out, they renewed their plotting. Georges Cadoudal,[4] Pichegru and other *émigrés* arrived secretly in Paris. The quiet Moreau, carried away by the proposals of his staff-officers who sought to make their General ambitious, persuaded himself that he was the First Consul's enemy and joined in the plot. There were meetings in Paris where plans were discussed for the assassination of Napoleon and the setting up of a new form of government.

[1] See Las Cases.
[2] Here Las Cases.
[3] The truth will be known later. In the meantime one may read the *Mémoires* of Count de Vauban, who was the General Lannes of the *émigrés*; as well as the pamphlets of M. de Montgaillard.
[4] Cadoudal's family has just been granted titles of nobility by H.M. Louis XVIII.

⌈ 25 ⌉

Pichegru and Georges were arrested.[1] Pichegru strangled himself in the prison of the Temple. Georges was executed. Moreau was tried and condemned to imprisonment. His sentence was commuted and he left for America. The Duke d'Enghien, a grandson of the Prince de Condé who lived in the territory of Baden, several miles beyond the French border, was arrested by the French police, brought to the prison of Vincennes, tried, condemned and executed as an *émigré* and conspirator. Of the lesser members of this conspiracy, some were executed while the majority were pardoned. The death sentence was commuted to one of imprisonment. Captain Wright, who had disembarked the conspirators and who appeared to have known their plans, was captured on the French coast, shut up for more than a year in the tower of the Temple, where he was so harshly treated that he put an end to his own life.

The discovery of this conspiracy procured Napoleon the last and greatest object of his ambition. He was made Emperor of the French, while the Empire was to be hereditary to his family.

'That fellow', remarked one of his own ambassadors, 'knows how to take advantage of everything.'

Such I believe to be the true story of these great events.[2] Once again I would point out that the whole truth about Bonaparte cannot possibly be known for at least a century. I have never found any proofs capable of withstanding the slightest scrutiny,[3]

---

[1] All that follows to be merged with Las Cases, 30th June, 1818.

[2] Furthermore: Napoleon must have felt the loss of Lucien acutely. He had become separated from him by a very natural feeling of jealousy as well as by the ascendancy of the Beauharnais set. Lucien possessed something that was lacking in Napoleon, and he would have prevented him from giving in to that fatal blindness which little by little caused him to become nothing more than an ordinary tyrant. *Biographies des hommes vivants*, Vol. L, p. 543.

[3] Never would greater benefits appear to have established greater claims. It would have been better for the happiness of France if Napoleon had died while engaged in monarchizing his admirable army at the Boulogne camp.—Dominique.

that Pichegru and Captain Wright met their deaths other than at their own hands.

What would have been Napoleon's motive for having Pichegru secretly killed? Since the iron character of the First Consul terrified Europe and France, the most impolitic thing he could do would be to give his enemies a pretext to accuse him of a crime. The army's affection for Pichegru had been diminished by his long absence and completely destroyed by a crime which in France, public opinion never forgives; that of openly trafficking with the nation's enemies. The most impartial Council of War would undoubtedly have condemned General Pichegru to death either as a traitor who had had connexions with the enemies of France, or for having conspired against the established government, or finally as a deportee who had returned to Republican territory. But, it may be objected, Pichegru had been put to the question. His thumbs had been pinched in the hammer of a gun, and Napoleon was afraid that this atrocity might become known. I would like to point out that the atrocious practice of putting people to the question has only been abolished in France since the Revolution, and that most of the crowned heads of Europe still employ it in cases of plotting against their persons. And finally, it is much better to run the risk of being accused of cruelty than of murder, while it would have been an easy matter to have thrown the blame on an inferior who could have been punished. It would have been possible for Pichegru to have been condemned to death by a decision that to the nation would have seemed just, and then to have had his sentence commuted to imprisonment for life. It may be observed that the expectation of obtaining a confession by torture had not been calculated for natures of Pichegru's type. As with a young brave, the cowardliness of the method employed would only have served to strengthen the dauntless character of the General. English and French prisoners in the Temple saw Pichegru's body, and no man worthy of confidence ever said he saw any trace of torture.

As for the affair of Captain Wright, it calls for a little more discussion. He was neither a traitor nor a spy. He openly served his country which was at war with France. The English say that when the Bourbons helped the pretenders of the House of Stuart in their repeated undertakings against the constitution and religion of England, their Government never treated with excessive severity any of the French engaged in these enterprises, who chanced to fall into their hands. When the fortunate issue of the Battle of Culloden, unlike that of Waterloo, quenched the last hopes of the English exiles, Frenchmen in the pay of the Pretender were made prisoners of war and treated exactly like prisoners taken in Flanders or Germany. My answer is that probably none of those French officers were captured while engaged in a murderous attempt upon the unlawful King of England. It may be asserted that Napoleon had Wright closely confined to prison with excessive severity, but after what had happened in Spain and France during the two previous years, there is no doubt but that legitimate kings would have treated the unhappy captain with even more revolting cruelty. There is nothing to prove that Napoleon had him put to death. What had he to gain from such a crime which, from his knowledge of the English press, would have resounded throughout the whole of Europe?

A very little thought will suffice to give direct proof of this. If the crime were in fact true, would we have to seek proof of it in 1818? Have all the gaolers who guarded Pichegru and Captain Wright already died? The police of France are in the hands of a man of superior intelligence, and such men have not been publicly interrogated. The same thing applies to men who would have been employed to murder Pichegru and Captain Wright. Is it for the sake of sparing Napoleon's reputation that the Bourbon government has not had recourse to this very simple measure? At the trial of the unfortunate General Bonnaire, there were soldiers who replied freely that they well remembered having fired on Gordon, to judges who could have had them shot in their turn.

AT SAINT HELENA, MR. WARDEN THE ENGLISH SURGEON, who would appear to have been a typical Englishman, that is to say a cold, narrow-minded and honest man, who hated Napoleon; one day told Napoleon that the truths of the Holy Gospel had not seemed more evident to him than his misdeeds. Carried away in spite of himself by the simplicity and greatness of soul of the man to whom he was speaking, Warden, abandoning all constraint, gave free reign to his feelings.[1] Napoleon appeared satisfied and in gratitude for his frankness inquired, to Warden's considerable astonishment, whether he remembered the story of Captain Wright.

'Perfectly well,' I replied, (wrote Warden in his *Memoirs*) 'and there isn't a single soul in England who does not believe that you had him put to death in the Temple.' He replied very sharply. ' With what object? Of all men, he was the one whose life was of most use to me. Where could I have found a more unimpeachable witness for the trial that was being prepared against the conspirators? It was he who had landed the leaders of the conspiracy upon the French coast. Listen,' continued Napoleon, 'and you shall learn all. Your Government sent a brig commanded by Captain Wright, which landed murderers and spies upon the west coast of France. Seventy of these people succeeded in reaching Paris and the whole business had been so cleverly carried out that although Count Réal of the Police, had told me of their arrival, their hiding-place could never be found. Each day I received fresh reports from my ministers informing me that there was to be an attempt upon my life and although I did not think the thing was as probable as they did, I took precautions for my safety.

'It so happened that the brig commanded by Captain Wright was captured not far from Lorient. This officer was taken before the Prefect of Morbihan, at Vannes. General Julien who at that

[1] P. 128, 6th edition, published by Ackerman (French ed.).

time was the Prefect, and who had been with me in Egypt, at once recognized Captain Wright. General Julien received orders to have each sailor or officer of the English ship's company questioned separately, and for these interrogations to be sent to the Ministry of Police.

'At first the interrogations appeared to be fairly insignificant. Nevertheless, at the end, the statement made by one member of the crew gave them what they sought. He said that the brig had landed several Frenchmen, and he particularly remembered one of them; very cheerful, and good company, called Pichegru. That one word uncovered a conspiracy which, had it succeeded would, for a second time, have plunged the French nation into the hazards of a revolution. Captain Wright was taken to the Temple. He was to have remained there until it was thought propitious to begin the trial of the conspirators. French law would have sent Captain Wright to the scaffold. But this was a detail of no importance. The essential was to make sure of the heads of the conspiracy.' The Emperor concluded by giving definite assurance several times that Captain Wright had taken his own life as stated in the *Moniteur*, and much earlier than was generally believed.

When on the Island of Elba, Lord Ebrington mentioned the death of Captain Wright to the Emperor, he did not at first remember the English name; but when he learned that he had been a companion of Sir Sidney Smith, he said: 'Did he then die in prison, because I have completely forgotten the circumstance?' He rejected all thought of a *coup d'état* and added that he had not caused any man to be put to death in a clandestine fashion and without a preliminary trial. 'My conscience is clear on this point. Had I felt less repugnance for bloodshed, perhaps I would not be here now.'

The evidence of M. de Maubreuil might lead one to believe that this dislike of murder is not so general as it is thought.[1]

[1] See the evidence of M. de Maubreuil, Marquis d'Aulay, taken down in shorthand and which is going around Paris in manuscript form.
Careful—more than careful.

WARDEN, THE ENGLISH SURGEON, TELLS HOW, TO HIS GREAT
astonishment after the story of Captain Wright, Napoleon began
to talk about the death of the Duke d'Enghien. He spoke rapidly,
frequently getting up from the sofa on which he was lying.

'At that period of my life, so full of incident,[1] I had succeeded
in restoring peace and order to an empire that had been rent
from top to bottom by factious parties and which was drenched
in blood. A great people had placed me at their head. Notice
that I did not reach the throne like your Cromwell or your
Richard III. Nothing of the kind. I found a crown in the gutter.
I wiped away the mud which covered it and placed it upon my
head. My life was indispensable to the continued existence of
the order which had been so recently restored, and which I had
successfully known how to preserve, as was recognized in
France by people who were leaders of opinion. At the time,
reports were brought to me every evening which informed me
that a conspiracy was being hatched, and that meetings were
taking place at private houses in Paris. Yet it was nevertheless
impossible to obtain satisfactory proof. All the vigilance of a
tireless police had been set at naught. My ministers even went
so far as to suspect General Moreau. They frequently urged me
to sign a warrant for his arrest. But at that time he had such a
great reputation in France that it seemed to me he had everything to lose and nothing to gain by plotting against me. I
refused the order for his arrest. I said to the Minister of
Police:

' "You have named Pichegru, Georges and Moreau to me,
prove that the first of these is in Paris and I will have the last one
arrested at once."

'A peculiar circumstance led to the discovery of the plot. One
night, when I was restless and unable to sleep, I got up and
began to look through the list of conspirators. Chance, which

[1] Warden, p. 144, of French ed.

after all rules the world, caused my eye to light upon the name of a surgeon recently returned from imprisonment in England. The man's age, education and experience of life gave me reason to think that his behaviour sprang from quite different motives than that of a young man's enthusiasm for the Bourbons. In so much as circumstances enabled me to judge, money was his aim. He was arrested and brought before police agents disguised as judges, by whom he was condemned to death, and he was informed that the sentence would be carried out within six hours. This trick produced its desired effect, and he confessed.

'It was known that Pichegru had a brother, an old monk living quietly in Paris. The monk was arrested and as the police were taking him away some words escaped him which finally revealed what I was so interested to learn: "It is because I gave shelter to a brother that I am treated like this."

'The first news of Pichegru's arrival in Paris had been given by a police spy who reported overhearing a curious conversation between Moreau, Pichegru and Georges, in a house on the boulevards. It had been agreed that Georges was to get rid of Bonaparte. Moreau was to be First Consul and Pichegru Second Consul. Georges insisted that he should be Third Consul. To this the others objected that since he was an acknowledged Royalist, any attempt on their part to associate him with the Government, would lose them all in the eyes of the public. Upon which the fiery Cadoudal cried: "Then if it is not to be me, I am for the Bourbons; and if it is to be neither for them nor for me, if it is to be a Republican, I would prefer it to be Bonaparte, rather than you."

'When Moreau was arrested and questioned he began by replying arrogantly, but when the official report of this conversation was shown to him, he fainted.

'The plot's object', continued Napoleon, 'was my death, and had it not been discovered it would have succeeded. This plot originated in the capital city of your country. The Count d'Angoumois was at the head of the whole affair.[1] He sent the

[1] Warden, p. 147.

52

Duke of Burgundy to the West[1] and the Duke d'Enghien to the East. Your ships unloaded the lesser members of the conspiracy upon the French coast. It might have been a crucial moment for me, and I felt my throne rock. I decided to return the thunder-bolt of the Barmecides,[2] even if it were to the very metropolis of the British Empire itself.

'My ministers urged me to have the Duke d'Enghien arrested although he was living on neutral territory. I continued to hesitate. Twice the Prince of Bén(évent) brought me the order for his arrest and, with all the energy of which he was capable, urged me to sign it. I was surrounded by murderers whom I was unable to discover. I did not give way until I was convinced that it was necessary.

'It was an easy matter to arrange with the Duke of Baden. Why should I have let an individual living on the frontiers of my Empire, freely commit a crime which, a mile nearer to me, would have led him to the scaffold? In this circumstance did I not perceive the principle on which your government acted when it ordered the taking of the Danish fleet? I had it dinned into my ears that the new dynasty could never be established so long as a single Bourbon remained. Talleyrand never swerved from this principle. It was the foundation, the very corner-stone of his political creed. I examined the idea with great attention, and the result of my reflexions was to cause me entirely to agree with Talleyrand. A proper right to defend my person, a proper right to care for public order,[3] caused me to decide against the Duke d'Enghien. I gave orders for him to be arrested and tried. He was condemned to death and shot, which was no more than would have happened had he been Louis IX himself.[4] From London, assassins had been sent against me, with the Count d'Angoumois (d'Artois) at their head. Are not any measures legitimate against assassination?'

[1] M. Royer points out that it was caution which caused Stendhal to disguise the names of Count d'Artois and of the Duke of Berry.

[2] The Bourbons, of course. Editor's note.

[3] See the massacres at Nîmes. The best account is that of a Protestant minister at London, M . . . See *Lyons in 1817*, by Colonel Fabvier.

[4] Warden, 6th ed. (French), p. 149.

[28]

Justification for this murder as such, actually cannot come from anything except proof that the young prince had taken part in the conspiracy against Napoleon's life. Such proof was referred to in the sentence pronounced at Vincennes, but was never made public. Here is another account given by Napoleon to Lord Ebrington:

'The Duke d'Enghien was engaged in a plot against my life. He had made two trips to Strasbourg in disguise. In consequence I gave orders for him to be seized and tried by a military commission which condemned him to death. I was told that he asked to speak with me, which affected me, because I knew him to be a young man of value and of good heart. I even think I might have seen him, but M. de Talleyrand prevented me from doing so by saying:

' "Don't go compromising yourself with a Bourbon. You don't know what the consequence may be. The thing is done now and we must go through with it." '

Upon Lord Ebrington inquiring whether it were true that the Duke had been shot by artificial light, the Emperor replied shortly:

'Oh no, that would have been against the law. The execution took place at the customary hour, and I gave orders for the report on the execution and the sentence to be posted up immediately in every town in France.'

It is remarkable, that in this and in other conversations on the same subject, Napoleon always appeared to think that to have seen the Duke and to have pardoned him were one and the same thing. James II, who was a very pious king, did not think so when he granted an audience to his brother's favourite son, with the fixed determination of having his head cut off when he left his room. This is because clemency is always closely allied to great courage.

'YOUR COUNTRY ALSO ACCUSES ME OF PICHEGRU'S DEATH,' continued the Emperor.[1]

'The great majority of English people are firmly convinced that you had him strangled in the Temple,' replied Warden.

Napoleon replied heatedly:

'What sheer stupidity! An excellent proof of the way in which passion can obscure that sureness of judgement of which the English are so proud! Why commit a crime by killing a man that every law of his country would send to the scaffold? If it had been a question of Moreau, it would have been excusable of the English to think this. Had this general met his death in prison there would have been reason to doubt his suicide. Moreau was beloved by the army and the people. His death in the shadow of a prison would never have been forgiven me, however innocent of it I might have been.'

'Napoleon stopped speaking,' added Warden, 'and I replied:

' "One may agree with you, General, that at that period of your history stringent measures were necessary, but no one, I think, will undertake to justify the precipitate way in which the young Duke d'Enghien was kidnapped, tried and executed."

'He replied hotly:

' "In my own opinion I was justified, and I repeat the statement I have already made, that I would have ordered the execution of Louis IX[2] quite as cold-bloodedly. Why did they seek to assassinate me? Since when is it forbidden to open fire upon a murderer who tries to shoot one? I swear with equal solemnity, that no message or letter from the Duke d'Enghien reached me after he had been condemned." '

Mr. Warden added:

---

[1] Georges, Pichegru, Moreau; here is a second justification of one of Napoleon's acts which takes up too much space. In the same way the facts which provoked it contain a great deal of repetition and verbosity. (Note by Vismara.)

True. (Note by Stendhal.)

[2] He means Louis XVIII. (Ed. note.)

'It is said that there exists a letter from the young prince to Napoleon, which is in the hands of M. de Talleyrand; but that the Minister took it upon himself not to deliver it until the hand which penned it was already cold. I have seen a copy of this letter in the possession of Count Las Cases. He showed it to me quite coldly, as being part of the pile of secret documents capable of proving certain mysterious points of the history he was writing at Napoleon's dictation.

'The young Prince asked for his life. He said that in his opinion the Bourbon dynasty was at an end. That such was his firm belief. He only looked upon France as his country and as such he cherished it with the true ardour of a patriot, but that all his feelings were those of a mere citizen. The prospect of a crown played no part in his conduct, as it was forever lost to the ancient dynasty. He therefore begged leave to devote his life and services to France, solely on his standing as a Frenchman born in France. He was prepared to accept any type of command in the French Army and to become a brave and loyal soldier, completely amenable to the orders of the government in which-ever hands it might find itself. He was prepared to take an oath of allegiance. He concluded by saying that if his life were spared, he would devote it with courage and unswerving fidelity to defending France against her enemies.'

[30]

Napoleon continued to talk of the Barmecide family.[1]

'Had I cherished the desire to have all the B . . . in my power, or any one member of this family, I could easily have done so. Your smugglers [in English in the text] offered me a B . . . for 40,000 francs. But when one reached a more definite understanding, they did not absolutely guarantee to hand over a

[1] The name which Stendhal prudently gave to the Bourbons. (Ed. note.)

living B . . . But on condition of dead or alive, they had no doubts about being able to fulfil their engagement. However, it was not solely my aim to deprive them of life. Circumstances had so well resolved themselves about me, that I felt sure of my throne. I was aware of my peace of mind, and I accorded peace of mind to the B . . . Whatever else may have been said about me in England, to kill for the sake of killing was never one of my maxims. To what end would I have entertained such a horrible point of view? When Sir George Rumbold and Mr. Drake, who were used to maintain contact with the conspirators in Paris, were taken prisoner, they were not put to death.'

[31]

I did not interrupt Napoleon's story. Two thoughts came to my mind. On the subject of Pichegru it may be said that all justification is founded upon the old principle of:

'He commits the crime, whom the crime serves.'

But is tyranny never the victim of inexplicable whims? All these arguments would be equally good in proving that Napoleon never threatened to have MM. Laîné, Flaugergues and Renouard shot!

On the subject of the death of the Duke d'Enghien, in ten years' time one may ask by just how many degrees it was more unjust than that of the Duke d'El(chingen)?[1] At the time of the death of the Duke d'Enghien it was said at court that his life had been sacrificed to the apprehensions of the buyers of national properties. I have it from General Duroc, that the Empress Josephine threw herself at Napoleon's feet to intercede for the Duke. Napoleon pushed her aside in a temper and left the room. She dragged herself on her knees as far as the door. During the night she wrote him two letters; her kind heart was really in a torment. At court I have heard it said that the aide-de-camp of

[1] Careful.

Marshal Moncey, the one who brought the news that the Duke had visited Strasbourg in disguise, had been misled. The young prince was carrying on an intrigue in Baden with a woman whom he did not wish to compromise, and so as to be able to meet her, from time to time he would disappear, or else he would live for seven or eight days in the cellar of the house in which the lady lived. During these absences it was thought that he had gone to Strasbourg to plot. It was this circumstance above all that had decided the Emperor. The *Mémoires* of Count Réal, of Count Lavalette and of the Dukes of Rovigo and of Vicenza will clarify all this. In any case, Napoleon would have spared himself a painful justification towards posterity if, before having the Duke d'Enghien arrested, he had waited for him to go to Strasbourg for a third time.

It may be asked whether freedom of the Press would ever have harmed the First Consul as much as did his subservience in the matter of the conspiracy of 1804. No one believed the story of the conspiracy at all. The First Consul was considered to have gratuitously assassinated the Duke d'Enghien and to have thought himself so ill-established as to have been afraid of Moreau's influence. Despite these drawbacks I think that Napoleon, the tyrant, did well to fetter the Press. The French nation enjoys a most fortunate peculiarity. In France, the great majority of thinking people consists of small landowners with an annual income of twenty louis. Nowadays this class alone possesses the energy which has been destroyed by good manners in the higher ranks of society. In the long run this class only understands and believes what it sees in print. The talk of the fashionable world dies out before it reaches it or soon fades from its memory. On the whole there was only one way of making this class aware of what it had not seen in print, and that was to arouse its fears on the subject of the national properties. As for Moreau, this general should have been put to use. He should have been placed in circumstances that would have fully exposed his weaknesses. For instance, to have caused him to lose his reputation during an expedition like that of Masséna's in Portugal.

PLANS FOR THE INVASION OF ENGLAND WERE DROPPED BE-
cause in the navy the Emperor failed to find those admirable
gifts which the Revolution had aroused in the ranks of the army.
It was a curious thing, but French officers appeared to lack
character.

Through conscription, the Emperor had *an annual intake of
eighty thousand men.*[1] With hospital wastage that was sufficient
for four big battles a year. In four years the invasion of England
could have been attempted eight times, and for anyone familiar
with the vagaries of the sea, one of these landings might well
have succeeded. Look at the French fleet which left Toulon,
took Malta and then arrived in Egypt. Ireland, oppressed by
the most abominable and bloody tyranny,[2] might quite possibly
have welcomed the foreigners in an access of despair.

On setting foot in England, the estates of the three hundred
peers were to have been divided among the poor. The constitution of the United States of America was to have been proclaimed, the English authorities were to have been organized,
Jacobinism was to have been encouraged. It was to have been
declared that the French had been called in by the oppressed
sections of the population; that they only sought to destroy a
government as harmful to France as it was to England, and that
they were prepared to withdraw. If, against every appearance,
a nation, one-third of which was living on charity, disregarded
this language some of which was sincere, the forty most important cities were to be burned down. It was highly probable
that fifteen million people of which a fifth had been pushed to

---

[1] In 1788, under the old régime, France had 25 million inhabitants. In 1818 she
had over 29 millions. This was because the number of men is always in proportion
to the number of grains of wheat. See the appendix to the work on France of M.
Le Sur, Paris, end of 1817. This appendix is supplied by the ministeries.

[2] See the *Edinburgh Review*, Nos. 56 or 55. As a matter of fact it is No. 54 to
which Stendhal refers here. To an article on the Catholic question in Ireland. (Ed.
note.)

extremity by the Government, and all of whom possessed courage but no military experience, would after two or three years have been unable to withstand thirty million men who, with a fair amount of enjoyment, obeyed a tyrant who was at the same time a man of genius.

All this failed to take place because our navy did not possess a Nelson[1]: the French army left the camp at Boulogne for a continental war that was to confer fresh brilliance upon the military reputation of the Emperor, and to raise him to a peak of greatness such as Europe had not seen accorded to any sovereign since the time of Charlemagne. For a second time Napoleon defeated the House of Austria and committed the mistake of sparing it. He only deprived it of its Venetian States, and obliged Emperor Franz to renounce his Imperial title and the influence which in Germany it still conferred upon him. The Battle of Austerlitz is probably a masterpiece of its kind.

The people noticed in amazement that the victory was won on December 2nd, the anniversary of Napoleon's coronation. From then on, no one in France was any longer shocked by that absurd ceremony.

⌈ 33 ⌉

THE FOLLOWING YEAR THE EMPEROR DEFEATED PRUSSIA, which had not had the courage to join with Austria and Russia. There was no other example in history where an army of two hundred thousand was wiped out in a single battle which gained the victor a great kingdom. This was because Napoleon understood even better how to take advantage of a victory, than how to inflict a defeat. At Jena on October 16th, not without some qualms, he attacked that army which had seemed to be sustained by the mighty ghost of Frederick. On October 26th, Napoleon entered Berlin.[2] To our considerable amazement the band

[1] Neither a Nelson, not a Lord Cochrane. See the story of Admiral Villeneuve
[2] Jena, October 14th. Napoleon made his entry into Berlin October 27th (Ed. note.)

played the Republican air: *Allons, enfants de la patrie*. For the first time, Napoleon, wearing the uniform of a general and with an embroidered hat, rode his horse twenty feet in front of his troops in the midst of the crowd. Nothing could have been easier than to have shot at him from one of the windows of the Unter den Linden.

It is sad to have to add that the silent crowd did not greet him with a single cheer.

For the first time the Emperor returned from his conquest with money. Over and above the upkeep of the army and its equipment, Austria and Prussia each paid out one hundred millions. The Emperor was hard on Prussia. He discovered that the German people were the finest in the world to conquer. A hundred Germans were always to be found on their knees before a uniform. That is what the finicky despotism of four hundred princes had done to the descendants of Arminius and of Vitiking.

It was then that Napoleon made the mistake that was to cost him his throne. Nothing would have been easier than for him to have placed whom he wished upon the thrones of Prussia and Austria. He could also have given both those countries a goverment of two chambers, with a semi-liberal constitution. He abandoned the old Jacobin principle of finding allies against the king in the very hearts of their own subjects. As a newly made king, he was already cultivating in the heart of the people a respect for the throne.

People around him knew that the voice of the man in the street had told him which princes to raise to the crown; this meant a great deal. The German peoples would then have tasted liberty. They would have used their strength to obtain an entirely liberal constitution, and, at the end of three or four years they would have felt a profound feeling of gratitude for him. There would then have been no *Tugenbund*, no more *Land-wehr*, no more burning zeal. On their side the new sovereigns would no longer have possessed either the strength or the will to allow themselves to be bribed by England into forming a coalition against France.

61

[34]

AT TILSIT NAPOLEON EXACTED NOTHING OF RUSSIA EXCEPT that she should close her ports to England. He was master of the Russian army, for Czar Alexander says himself that he had ended the war because he lacked muskets. The Russian army so imposing today, was then in a piteous state.[1] It was lucky for the Czar that the Emperor had conceived the Continental System at Berlin. Alexander and Napoleon had the most intimate conversations and discussions that would have surprised their subjects greatly had they been in a position to overhear them.

'During the two weeks we spent together at Tilsit,' said Napoleon, 'we dined together almost every day. We rose early from table so as to be rid of the King of Prussia, who bored us. At nine o'clock the Emperor, in plain clothes, came to take tea with me. We remained together, talking casually of various subjects, until two or three in the morning. As a general rule we talked politics and philosophy. The Czar is well-informed, and holds liberal opinions. He owed all that to his tutor Colonel Laharpe. I was occasionally hard put to it to know whether the sentiments he expressed were his real opinions or the result of that vanity, common in France, of taking up a point of view in contrast to one's position.'

In one of these *tête-à-têtes*, the two Emperors discussed the comparative advantages of the hereditary and the elective monarchies. The hereditary despot was for the elective monarchy, while the soldier of fortune was for the hereditary order.

'How small a hope there is that a man, whom the chances of birth have placed on the throne, will possess the talents required to rule.'

'How few men', replied Napoleon, 'have possessed those qualities which give them the right to such high distinction. A

---

[1] See the pamphlet by General Wilson, published in 1806.*

*The pamphlet by General Wilson, M. Royer points out, dates from 1817. (Ed. note.)

Caesar or an Alexander. There is not one in a whole century. After all, an election is also a question of luck, and rule by succession is surely to be preferred to the throw of the dice.'

Napoleon left the north, firmly convinced that he had made a friend of Czar Alexander, which was rather ridiculous. But it is a great mistake of a kind that rightly confounds his detractors. At the same time it proves that he was unsuited to politics. With a pen in hand he always undid what he had accomplished with the sword. While passing through Milan, he discussed the Continental System with Melzi. It was then with good reason his favourite aim. This idea was of more value than the whole of Cardinal Richelieu's life. It almost succeeded and at present the whole of Europe is taking it up again.[1]

Melzi pointed out to him that Russia possessed raw materials but no manufactured goods, and that it was unlikely that the Czar would long remain faithful to a measure which so openly offended against the interests of the nobility, in a country where those interests were so opposed to the sovereign. To which Napoleon replied that he counted upon the personal friendship which he had inspired in Alexander.[2] This idea staggered the Italian. Napoleon had just told him an anecdote which proved how little one could count on the power of Alexander, even if he had been favourably disposed towards France. At Tilsit Napoleon treated General Beningsen with special consideration. Alexander noticed this and asked the reason.

'Quite frankly,' replied Napoleon, 'it is a tribute to you. You have entrusted your army to him and it is enough that he enjoys your confidence for me to be filled with friendship and consideration towards him.'

[1] Another year of perseverance and it would have succeeded.
[2] For the rest of this passage see *The Edinburgh Review*, No. 54, p. 486.

[35]

THE TWO EMPERORS, OF THE SOUTH AND THE NORTH, SAW
each other at Erfurt.[1] Austria realized her peril and attacked
France. Napoleon left Paris on April 13th, 1809; by the 18th he
was at Ingolstadt. He fought six battles in five days and won six
victories. On May 10th he was at the gates of Vienna. Nevertheless, the army, already corrupted by despotism, did not do as
well as it had done at Austerlitz.

If the general in command of the Austrian army had cared to
follow up the proposal put forward, it is said, by General Belle-
garde, Napoleon might have been taken prisoner through having unwisely crossed the Danube at Essling. He was saved by
Marshal Masséna. He made him a prince, but at the same time
he meant to humiliate him by conferring upon him the name of
a lost battle; in giving him the title of Prince of Essling. The
pettiness of a court is already apparent. How can nations be
expected to interpret such an honour?

Austria employed a stroke of good policy. She appealed to
public opinion and protected the revolt in the Tyrol. General
Chasteller distinguished himself sufficiently for the tyrant to
pay him the honour of wreaking upon him his impotent wrath.
The *Moniteur* called him the *infamous* Chasteller. In 1809 in the
mountains of the Tyrol this same general began what the
sociétés de la vertu were to accomplish in 1813, on the battlefields of Leipzig.

Between the Battle of Essling and the victory at Wagram,
the French Army was concentrated inside Vienna.[2] The revolt in
the Tyrol deprived it of the means of subsistence. The army had
seventy thousand sick and wounded. It was a great achievement
on the part of Count Daru to have fed the army under these conditions, but this *tour de force* was never referred to because it
would have meant admitting the danger. During this interval,

---

[1] Nothing positive is known about the details of the meeting at Erfurt.
[2] From May 22nd to July 6th, 1809.

which might have proved so fatal, Prussia dared not make a move.

One of the facts which most justifies what is at present taking place at Saint Helena, if anything unjust may ever be justified, was the death of Palm, the bookseller. The Emperor had him murdered by a council of war, not far from Jena, but although tyranny can do much with impunity, it cannot destroy the printed word. If it were given the means, the throne and the altar might once again hope for a return to the happy days of the Middle Ages.

A student from Jena, with a volume of Schiller in his pocket, came to Schönbrunn to assassinate Napoleon. He was in uniform with his right arm in a sling and with this arm he held a dagger. The student mingled easily with the crowd of wounded officers who had come to ask for compensation. But the sombre insistence with which he demanded to see the Emperor and his refusal to give an account of himself to the Prince of Neuchâtel, who interrogated him, caused the Prince to have him arrested. He confessed everything. Napoleon wished to spare him and asked him the following question:

'What will you do if you are given your freedom.'

'Try and do it again.'

The Battle of Wagram was splendid. Four hundred thousand men fought all day. Struck by the bravery of the Hungarians and remembering their national feelings, Napoleon toyed for a time with the idea of making Hungary into an independent kingdom, but he was afraid of neglecting Spain, and, furthermore, he never saw the full scope of this idea.

For some time sycophants surrounding him had pointed out that he owed it to his dynasty to select a wife who would give him a son, from among the European royal families. At Schönbrunn the idea was mooted of having him marry an Archduchess. He was extremely flattered. On April 2nd, 1810, he received the hand of the daughter of the Caesars. The day, the most glorious of his life, he was as gloomy as Nero. He was galled by the quips of the Parisians [never did Archduchess make so vile (*si vil*[1]) a marriage] and by the cardinal's resistance. On March 20th, 1811, he had a son; Napoleon-François-Charles Joseph. This event won him the nation's eternal devotion. In Paris enthusiasm reached its peak at the twenty-first salute of cannon. This people, so chilled by the fear of ridicule, shouted their applause in the streets. Throughout the countryside there was more talk than ever of the Emperor's lucky star. The prestige of Fate was his.

Since he gave up being the *son of the Revolution* wanting to be nothing more than a mere sovereign, repudiating the support of the nation, it was just as well for him to make sure of the support of the most illustrious family in Europe.[2] How different it would have been for him, had he allied himself with Russia!

[36]

ON SPAIN

THE EVENING OF THE DAY ON WHICH THE BATTLE OF JENA was fought, Napoleon was still upon the battlefield when he received the Prince of Peace's proclamation calling all Spaniards to arms. Napoleon was acutely aware of the peril from which he had just escaped. He saw to what alarums the south of France would be exposed at each new expedition which he might undertake in the north. He determined not to leave in his rear a treacherous friend ready to attack him as soon as he thought he was entangled. He remembered that at Austerlitz he had found the King of Naples among his enemies two weeks after he had signed a peace with his court. The way in which the Prince of Peace planned to attack France was contrary to international law as it appears to have been adopted by modern nations. M. de Talleyrand did not stop repeating to Napoleon that there would be no security for his dynasty until he had wiped out the Bour-

---

[1] Translator's note: *Si vil*—a pun on civil marriage—a non-religious ceremony.
[2] Ironical for 1814.

bons. To dethrone them was not enough; yet one had to begin by dethroning them.

At Tilsit Russia approved the Emperor's plans for Spain. These plans consisted in giving Don Manuel Godoy, well known as the Prince of Peace, a principality in the Algarves. In return for this the Prince, sole author of the proclamation which lost Spain, was to deliver up his king and benefactor to Napoleon. Under the terms of the Treaty of Fontainebleau concluded by the Prince of Peace, Spain was overrun by Imperial troops. Ultimately this favourite, as powerful as he was absurd, realized that Napoleon was making fun of him. He thought of fleeing to Mexico. The people wished to keep their king, and from this arose the events of Aranjuez which called Ferdinand VII to the throne and overthrew Napoleon's plan. On March 18th, 1808, this very stupid and very brave people revolted. The Prince of Peace, who was loathed quite as much as he deserved, passed from supreme power into prison. A second rising forced King Charles IV to abdicate in favour of Ferdinand VII. Napoleon was very much surprised. He had thought he was treating with Prussians or Austrians, and that to have disposed of the court, meant disposing of the nation as well. Instead of which he found a nation with a young prince at its head whom it adored, and who was apparently alien to the degradation which had weighed over Spain for the past fifteen years. This prince might possess the facile virtues of his rank, and be surrounded by men of integrity who were devoted to the country, impervious to bribery, and sustained by a people to whom fear was unknown. All that Napoleon knew about the Prince of Asturias was that in 1807 he had dared to write asking him for the hand in marriage of one of his nieces, a daughter of Lucien Bonaparte.

After the events at Aranjuez, all classes of the Spanish population were filled with enthusiasm. Yet the foreigner at the very heart of the state, still held command in the capital, occupied the garrison towns and was the real judge between Ferdinand VII and King Charles IV who had just revoked his abdication and called on Napoleon for help.

In this unique position, by a fresh stroke of the argumentative ineptitude characteristic of the ministers of a nation long detached from European progress, Ferdinand VII resolved to go to meet Napoleon. General Savary made two trips to Spain to urge the prince to come to Bayonne, but he never offered to recognize his title. The new king's advisers, who feared the vengeance of Charles IV against whom they had conspired, saw no security except with Napoleon, and yearned to reach him with their prince.

Seen from afar, these great events look curious, but a closer inspection reveals them to be merely disgusting. Spanish ministers are too stupid, and French agents too astute. It is the old, stupidly treacherous policy of Philip II fighting against the wholly modern genius of Napoleon.[1] There were two redeeming features. M. Hervas, brother of the Duchess of Frioul, at danger to more than his life, reached Vallodolid and did everything humanly possible to open the eyes of the stupidly self-important ministers of Ferdinand VII. The general in command of the frontier guards on the line of the Ebro, a brave and simple man, suggested to Ferdinand that he should kidnap him with the two thousand men at his disposal; and received a severe reprimand. That was typical of Spain's behaviour during the next six years. Stupidity, meanness and cowardice on the part of its princes; and a romantic and heroic devotion on the part of the people.

Ferdinand VII reached Bayonne the morning of April 20th, where he was greeted as a king. In the evening, General Savary came to inform him that Napoleon had decided to place his own dynasty upon the Spanish throne. In consequence, Napoleon demanded that Ferdinand VII should abdicate in his favour. At that very moment the Emperor was having that curious conversation with the Spanish Minister Escoïquiz, in which his character is so admirably revealed as well as his entire policy towards Spain.[2]

[1] See the book by M. Escoïquiz.
[2] See the works of MM. Escoïquiz and de Pradt, of which this is only an extract.

Napoleon's plan was defective in that it offered Etruria and Portugal to the princes who had been hunted out of Spain. This left power in the hands of his enemies.

Ferdinand VII, victim of a base favourite, a blind father, an idiotic council and a powerful neighbour, was in fact a prisoner at Bayonne. How was he to escape from such a tight corner? Short of taking wing, there was no possibility of escape, so good were the precautions which had been taken. Each day they were reinforced. Day and night the ramparts of the town swarmed with soldiers, the gates were closely guarded, every face was scrutinized at entry and departure. There were rumours of attempts at escape and surveillance became even more active. It was open captivity. Nevertheless Ferdinand's council firmly refused to accept Etruria in exchange for Spain.

The Emperor was a prey to the most violent agitation and even to remorse. He saw Europe reproaching him with keeping prisoner a prince who had come to confer with him. He was as much embarrassed at keeping Ferdinand as at releasing him. He found himself in the position of having committed a crime and of losing what he had gained by it. He said to the Spanish ministers with great truth and energy:

'You should adopt more liberal ideas; be less touchy on points of honour and not sacrifice the prosperity of Europe to the interests of the Bourbon family.'

But the ministers who had led Ferdinand VII to Bayonne, were not of a calibre to conceive such ideas. Compare Spain as it has been for the last four years; happy in its abjection, the object of the contempt or abhorrence of other nations, with a Spain equipped with the two Chambers, and with Joseph for constitutional king. So much better a king in that, like Bernadotte, he had only his own worth in his favour, and at the first sign of injustice or stupidity, he could be dismissed and the legitimate king called in.

Never had Napoleon's mind known a more astounding activity. From one moment to the next fresh ideas would come to him which he immediately had proposed to the Spanish ministers. In such a state of anxiety man cannot simulate and it was possible to see deep into the heart and mind of the Emperor. He had the warm heart of a soldier, but a poor head for politics. The Spanish ministers who rejected everything with high-minded indignation, cut a fine figure. They always proceeded according to the principle that Ferdinand had no right to dispose of Spain without the consent of the nation.[1] Their refusals reduced Napoleon to despair. It was the first big opposition he had encountered, and in what circumstances! As it was, the absurd Spanish Council had achieved, through blindness, an enlightened act that was most awkward for its opponent. In this mortal anxiety, Napoleon's mind seized upon every kind of idea at once, and upon every sort of project. Several times a day he would call for his negotiators; he would send them to the Spanish ministers. But there were always the same answers, protests and refusals! Upon his ministers' return, Napoleon would go over with them, with his customary rapidity of imagination and speech, every aspect of the question. When he was told that there was no way of persuading the Prince of Asturias to accept the little kingdom of Etruria in exchange for the Spanish or American monarchies, that after having seen the first throne taken from him, the second must have appeared very precarious to him, he replied:

'Very well, let him declare war on me!'

Any man who is capable of such a singular sally is no Philip II, as some would have us believe. There was honour, great honour even, in such an expression of feeling which also contained much wisdom.

It is to be found again in the conversation published by M. Escoïquiz: 'Furthermore, if my proposals do not suit your Prince, he may, if he so desires, return to his States, but first of all we will together fix a date for this return after which hostilities will break out between us.'

One of the men whom Napoleon employed on these negotiations, claims to have raised objections to him about the very nature of the undertaking.

[1] A Jacobin principle that was rejected by the Congress of Vienna.

'Oh,' he said, 'I feel that what I am doing is not good, but let them then declare war upon me!'

The Emperor told his ministers: 'I must feel this enterprise to be very necessary to my peace of mind, because I am badly in need of ships, and this is going to cost me the six vessels I have at Cadiz.'

On another occasion: 'If this were to cost me eighty thousand men I would not do it. But it will not take twelve thousand, it is child's play. These people do not know what French troops are. The Prussians were like them once, and one has seen what happened to them.'

Nevertheless, after eight days of acute anxiety, since the negotiations had made no progress, a way out had to be found. Napoleon was not used to opposition. His was a nature ruined by tyranny and by an unheard of series of successes. He might have become ferocious through obstruction. It is said that one day the words 'fortress prison' escaped him. The following day he apologized to his ministers:

'You must not be offended by what you heard yesterday: I would surely not have done it.'

[37]

PERCEIVING THAT THERE WAS NOTHING TO HOPE FOR FROM the Prince of Asturias, Napoleon had the excellent idea of picking a quarrel with him over the validity of the abdication of Charles IV. This abdication had obviously been forced; and it had then been revoked.

The Prince of Peace was removed from his prison in Madrid and on April 26th he arrived at Bayonne. On May 1st, the *old rulers* as they were called by the Spaniards, arrived. The sight of them made a great impression. They were miserable, and ancient long-preserved ceremonial is mistaken for character by the common people.

As soon as the King and Queen of Spain had entered their apartments, the French saw all the Spaniards who happened to be in Bayonne, with Prince Ferdinand at their head, perform the ceremony of kissing hands, which entails kneeling down and kissing the hands of the King and Queen. Onlookers who had read that very morning in the *Gazette de Bayonne* documents relative to the events of Aranjuez and the King's protest, and who then saw this unhappy monarch receiving the homage of the very same men who had hatched the plot in March, were revolted by such duplicity and looked in vain for Castilian honour. The French were unwise enough to judge the Spanish nation by the higher ranks of society which, in sentiment, are everywhere the same.

After the ceremony, the Prince of Asturias wished to follow the *old rulers* into their private apartments. The King stopped him, saying in Spanish:

'Prince, have you not sufficiently insulted my white hairs?'

These words appeared to strike the rebellious son like a thunderbolt.[1]

⌈ 38 ⌉

THE KING AND QUEEN GAVE NAPOLEON AN ACCOUNT OF THE insults to which they had been subjected.

'You have no idea', they said, 'what it means to have cause to complain of a son.'

They also spoke of the contempt inspired in them by the bodyguards, the cowards who had betrayed them.

The French negotiators made it clearly understood to the Prince of Peace that there was no longer any question of continuing his rule in Spain.

Already on the day preceding the arrival of Charles IV, Napoleon had sent for M. Escoïquiz and had instructed him to inform the Prince of Asturias that all negotiations with him

[1] The *Moniteur* May 6th, 1808.

were broken off and that in future he would negotiate only with the King of Spain.

For Napoleon was now the absolute master of the wishes of the King of Spain through the intermediary of the Prince of Peace. The English have repeatedly said that violence was used as well as intrigue. The truth is that there were neither intriguers nor plotters, but, as usual, only idiots led and duped by rogues. There was also as usual, a foreign ruler who was defied in a manner that was absolutely contrary to international law, and who took advantage of it all.

[39]

WHILE KING CHARLES IV AT BAYONNE WAS ORDERING HIS son Ferdinand VII to return his crown to him, the people of Madrid, alarmed by such strange events which were moreover an insult to the entire nation in the person of their sovereign, revolted on May 2nd; some one hundred and fifty inhabitants and five hundred French soldiers perished. This news, greatly exaggerated, reached France on May 5th. Charles IV sent for his son. The King, the Queen, and Napoleon were seated, the Prince, who remained standing was overwhelmed by the most coarse abuse. Disgusted Napoleon remarked:

'I have just left them quarrelling like street porters.'

Intimidated, the Prince formally and definitively renounced the throne. On the same day, May 5th, 1808, King Charles IV ceded all his Spanish rights to Napoleon. The Prince of Asturias also ceded to Napoleon all his rights to the Spanish throne, but it is said, only after he had several times been threatened with death by the king, his father. There was the example of Don Carlos and, moreover, as the Prince had obviously conspired against his father and king, the most fair-minded jury in the world would have condemned him to death.

Napoleon has been accused of having gone so far as to tell him:

'Prince, you must choose between cession or death.'[1] It remains to be seen how this remark will be proved to posterity.

The Spanish Bourbons went to live in various cities. Everywhere and at every opportunity King Charles protested his affection and devotion to his august ally. No one has as yet accused Napoleon of threatening him. As for Ferdinand VII, he went to live on the beautiful estate of Valençay.

Here ends what are known as Napoleon's treacheries. Unable to believe that his enemies had been so faint-hearted, Europe held him criminally responsible for their stupidity.

Napoleon had sent General Savary to the Prince of Asturias to hasten his arrival, but he had never promised him recognition as king.[2] The Prince went to Bayonne because he always believed that it was in his interest to do so. He thought, possibly with reason, that only Napoleon could save him from his father and the Prince of Peace.

At Vittoria, April 13th, 1808, a Spanish minister, M. d'Urquijo, met the young king and his suite on their way to Bayonne. The same day he wrote to the Captain-General La Cuesta ' . . . I said to them (to Ferdinand's ministers) that for Napoleon it was merely a question of abolishing the Bourbon dynasty in Spain in imitation of Louis XIV's example, and of setting up that of France . . . L'Infantado, who felt the weight of my remarks, replied: "Is it possible that a hero like Napoleon would besmirch himself by such an action, when the king had placed himself in his hands in all good faith?" '

' "Read Plutarch," I told him, "and you will find that all those heroes of Greece and Rome only won their fame over thousands of dead bodies. All that is now forgotten, while the results remain to be contemplated with respect and astonishment."

' "I added that he should remember the crowns stolen by Charles V of Germany, the cruelties he perpetrated upon sovereigns and upon peoples and that in spite of it all he was

[1] Cevalhos, p. 52.
[2] 'Although your representatives constantly refused to recognize him as a legitimate sovereign.' (Conversation by Escoïquiz.)

74

numbered among the heroes. That he should also not forget that we had done as much to the emperors and kings of India . . . that he could apply the same thing to the origins of every dynasty in the world, and that in our own Spain of olden times kings were to be found murdered by usurpers who then placed themselves upon the throne. That in foregoing centuries in our own history there was the murder committed by the bastard Enrique II and the banning of the family of Henri IV; that the Austrian and Bourbon dynasties were derived from this incest as well as from these crimes . . . I said that the language used by the *Moniteur* had made it apparent to me that Napoleon did not recognize Ferdinand as king and said that his father's abdication, which had taken place under arms and in the midst of a rising of the people, was null and void, and that Charles IV would himself admit this. Also, that without referring to what had happened to Juan I, King of Castile, there were two other examples of abdication in the more modern Austrian and Bourbon dynasties; one by Charles V of Germany, the other by Philip V, and that both these abdications had taken place with great calm and judicious deliberation and even with the help of those who represented the nation." [1]

In the conversation with M. Escoïquiz, which up to the present is the most interesting document on this case, as well as the most authentic, because it was published by an enemy, Napoleon observed quite rightly:

'But, after all, the supreme law of rulers which is that of the good of their states, obliges me to do what I am doing.'

It should be pointed out, to the great surprise of the stupid, that a sovereign who is no more than a kind of attorney general, can never act generously or make free gifts. We will meet this problem again in Italy where it had been hoped that, contrary to what he believed to be the interests of France, Napoleon would have made the Italians a present of their complete independence.

[1] Faithfully copied from the book by M. Escoïquiz. Only books written by the Emperor's enemies are quoted here.

Unexpectedly attacked by Spain at a time when she thought him involved with Prussia, Napoleon was obliged at Bayonne to treat Spain in a way which he believed to be of greatest advantage to France. If he had been defeated at Jena, would not the Spaniards, led by the Lascys and the Porliers, have gone to Toulouse and Bordeaux, while the Prussians would have been in Strasbourg and Metz?

Posterity will decide whether it was a crime for the *attorney general* of a nation to have taken advantage of the extreme stupidity of his enemies. I believe that unlike our own times, posterity will be more struck by the wrongs meted out to Spain than by the wrongs done to its alleged masters. There is the example of Norway.

Slanderous writers accuse Napoleon of having had too great a contempt for mankind. Here we see him committing a grave error because he had too high an opinion of the Spanish people. He forgot that the proud Castilians, first debased by Charles V of Germany, have, since that famous Emperor, been governed by the most cowardly despotism.

M. d'Urquijo said in his letter to General La Cuesta:

'Unfortunately, since Charles V, the nation no longer exists, because there is no organized body of men which really represents it, nor any common interest that unites it to a single end. This Spain of ours is a Gothic edifice made up of bits and pieces having almost as many privileges, laws, customs and interests as it has provinces. Public spirit does not exist.'

For the past fifteen years, the Spanish monarchy has attained a degree of absurdity unheard of in the annals of the most degenerate courts. An aristocracy of nobles and priests which alone gives lustre to a monarchy, had allowed itself to be wantonly flouted. A husband and king, gave his wife's lover successively:

1. Supreme command over all land and sea forces.
2. The appointing of almost all public offices.
3. The right to declare war or to make peace on his own authority.[1]

1 Conversation published by Escoïquiz.

Had this favourite been a Richelieu, a Pombal, an Ximenes or a clever rogue, the Spaniards might have been understood. But it so happened that he was the most stupid rascal in Europe. This nation, which claimed to be so proud, saw itself ruled despotically by the very object of its contempt. But, setting aside all pride, such general as well as private misfortunes should not have produced so infamous a government! Our French aristocracy as it was prior to 1789, must have been republic compared with Spain. And yet Spain rejected a liberal constitution and furthermore, a constitution guaranteed by the proximity of the legitimate and deposed sovereign!

One must be well advanced in years and have as great a contempt for mankind as it deserves, to be able to conceive of such conduct. Napoleon, who had lived in Corsica and in France among people who were full of vigour and shrewdness was, with regard to the Spaniards, the dupe of his own heart.

Spain on her part, lost an opportunity which succeeding centuries will not offer her again. Every power has an interest (ill understood, to be sure) in seeing its neighbours in a state of weakness and of decadence. Here, by a unique stroke of luck, the interests of France and of the Peninsula coincided for a time. As an example, Spain could look to Italy which Napoleon had recreated. Although the Spanish nation is at present quite content upon its own dung-heap, in two hundred years' time perhaps it will have succeeded in obtaining a constitution; though one having no other guarantee than the old rigmarole of oaths, and God only knows at the cost of how much bloodshed it will have to be bought! Whereas, by accepting Joseph for king, the Spaniards would have had a kind man, full of learning and devoid of ambition, and who was a born constitutional king. They would then have advanced the happiness of their country by three centuries.

[40]

LET IT BE ASSUMED THAT FERDINAND VII HAD GIVEN HIM-
self up to the Emperor, as Napoleon gave himself up to the
English at Rochefort. The Spanish Prince refused the Kingdom
of Etruria, and he was conducted to Valençay, a pleasant and
healthy spot, while Napoleon, who had appealed to the greatly
vaunted generosity of the English people, was imprisoned upon
a rock where, by indirect means and by avoiding the odium of
poison, they tried to do away with him. I do not say that the
English nation is worse than any other; I will only point out
that Heaven gave her a most unfortunate opportunity of showing how base she was.

And in fact what an outcry there was at this great crime!
What a generous outburst of feeling by an entire people upon
learning of this abominable act which, in the eyes of other
nations, served to repudiate its government! Oh Saint Helena,
rock forever famed! You are the reef on which the glory of
England was shipwrecked! Setting herself above other peoples
by a misleading hypocrisy, she yet dared to boast of her virtues;[1]
this great act unmasked her; now let her only boast of her
victories for so long as she continues to have any. Europe nevertheless remains silent and accuses Napoleon, or at least she
appears to listen to those who accuse him. I cannot say what I
think. Oh cowardly and jealous men, is it possible to despise you
too much? And when one fails to master you, is it not wise to
bait you as though you were some loathsome animal?

[1] See General Bertrand's letter to Sir Hudson Lowe. *Documents relative to the
prisoner of Saint-Helena*, London, 1818. See the hypocritical speech of Lord Bathurst
in the *Letters of Dr. O'Meara*.

[41]

Let us end in a few words this disgusting Spanish business.

In the conversation at Bayonne, Escoïquiz said to Napoleon: 'The unarmed people of Madrid thought they were strong enough to destroy the French army and protect Ferdinand. To such an extent in fact, that insuperable obstacles would have been presented in the event of their having sought to use the only means of placing Ferdinand at liberty.'

Napoleon: 'What then was the only means, Canon?'

Escoïquiz: 'That of having the king flee in secret.'

Napoleon: 'And to which part of the world would you have taken him?'

Escoïquiz: 'To Algeciras, where we already had some troops and where we would have been close to Gibraltar.'

Napoleon: 'And afterwards, what would you have done?'

Escoïquiz: 'True to our invariable principle of preserving a close and at the same time an honourable alliance with Your Majesty, we would have proposed peremptorily to continue it on condition that our frontiers were restored to us without delay, and that the French troops left Spain. In the event of Your Majesty refusing to agree to these proposals, we would have made war upon you with all our might and to the very end. Such would have been my opinion, Sire, in the event of our having by one means or another known your real intentions!'

Napoleon: 'You reason extremely well. That was quite the best you could have done.'

The ill-informed will exclaim: 'With regard to Spain you praise Napoleon as though he had been a Washington.'

To which I would reply: 'Spain met the most fortunate opportunity to be granted to a nation that was profoundly corrupt and therefore in no state to bestow freedom upon itself. To have given the Spain of 1808 a government similar to that of the United States would have seemed to the Spaniards, who are the

79

most inconsequential of men, like a harsh and painful tyranny. The experiences of Joseph and Joachim at Naples clarify the question. They had been kings with nearly all the absurd trappings of the trade, yet they were moderate and reasonable. It was enough, in those countries, to speed the advance of happiness and justice, and to begin to make work respected. It should be pointed out that the painful sensations an individual feels when breaking himself of bad habits, are also felt by a nation. Liberty needs to be handled carefully during the early years, and to the stupid such constraint disguises the benefits that are to be derived from new institutions.

Therefore, in the case of Spain, Napoleon was better than Washington. What he lacked in generosity, he made up in vigour. There was one fact, obvious even to people who never perceived moral factors; the population of Spain which was only eight million when Philip II entered it, was increased to twelve million by the small amount of French common sense introduced by the kings of that nation. Spain, which is larger than France, should be more fertile on account of her sun; while she enjoys almost all the advantages of an island. What, therefore, is the unknown force which hinders the birth of fourteen million men? To which it will be replied: 'The lack of cultivated land.' And for my part I would say: 'What unknown poison prevents the land from being cultivated?'

After the cession of Spain by princes of a dynasty which war had placed upon the throne ninety years before, Napoleon wished to convene an Assembly, to have it recognize his rights and to draw up a constitution, and by means of the weight and prestige of his authority, to set the new machine in motion.

Of all European countries Spain was perhaps the one in which Napoleon was most admired. Compare his methods with those of Louis XIV in 1713. Above all consult the correspondence of the lesser people of both periods: ministers, marshals, generals, etc. . . .[1] You will be forced to admit that envy was the main reason for the success of Mme. de Staël and the modern author

[1] See Saint-Simon, le Marquis de Saint-Philippe, *Memoirs of Marshal de* . . .

of libels, and for the perils and ridicule which the base and vulgar herd lavish upon all who defend the prisoner of Saint Helena.

So that the rights of the new king should derive from the rights of the people, at Bayonne Napoleon sought to form a *Convention* of one hundred and fifty members taken from among the various bodies attached to the monarchy. The majority of the deputies were nominated by the provinces, towns and corporations. The others were appointed by the French general in command at Madrid (Murat, Grand-Duke of Berg). In all this, as in every revolution, there was nothing wholly legal, because how could the political customs of a people, which are still called its constitution, furnish rules on which to base a change of dynasty? That is an implied contradiction. Everything was effected by the troubled and swift-moving events, but all in all, they remained faithful to the true principles. For example, who had the right to nominate the American representatives? They took what they found from among the most outstanding Americans living in Madrid, and the choice happened to be an excellent one. For they were less oppressed by preconceived ideas than the Spaniards.

The Junta began its sittings on June 15th, 1808. It consisted of seventy-five members, later increased to ninety. This meeting had been preceded by a decree issued by Napoleon which stated that due to representations made by the leading authorities in Spain, he had decided, so as to put an end to the interregnum, to proclaim his brother Joseph King of the Two Spains and of India and to guarantee the independence and integrity of the monarchy in the four corners of the earth.[1]

Joseph reached Bayonne on June 7th. He left regretfully the voluptuous life which he had created for himself at Naples. As fine a man as Philip V, he was no more of a general than that prince had been.

The deputies assembled at Bayonne recognized Joseph as King on the evening of June 7th. As the speech of the Duke of

[1] The *Moniteur* of June 18th, 1808.

81

Infantado failed to express definite recognition, Napoleon exclaimed:

'There must be no evasiveness, monsieur. You must recognize him unreservedly or else refuse in the same way. One must be as great in sin as in virtue. Do you want to return to Spain and place yourself at the head of the insurgents? I give you my word that I will have you conducted back there in safety, but I can assure you that you will behave in such a manner as to get yourself shot within a week . . . no, within twenty-four hours.'[1]

Napoleon was too clever and too generous to fulfil this threat. In the language of the French army, it was known as *emporter son homme par la blague* (to talk a man into doing something) which means to confuse a weak character.

At the end of twelve sessions the Convention finished its work on July 7th. It had drawn up a constitution for Spain. The draft of this constitution had been sent from Bayonne to the government Junta at Madrid. Sent back to Bayonne, the act was further increased by a considerable number of new articles, since from the eighty it had contained at Madrid, it finally reached one hundred and fifty.

In the first place according to established principles, it will be seen that the convention had been charged with drawing up a constitution while remaining absolutely separate from the body governing it. It was the lack of this precaution which lost France in 1792.

Members of the Bayonne convention had no taste for martyrdom, as was to be seen from their speeches to King Joseph. Nevertheless they proceeded with a delicacy which appeared to promise considerable freedom. Considering themselves to be no longer competent to order the expulsion of one dynasty and the declaration of another, they never even discussed this essential matter.

[1] See the speech of the Duke of Infantado in the *Moniteur* of June 18th. The Castilian hero forebears of M. le Duc, would have had some difficulty in recognizing themselves.

The deputies agreed in admitting that no restrictions had been placed upon the freedom of their debates. The obstinacy with which the Spanish grandees maintained the illiberal right to form large entailed properties, shows to what extent they believed in the stability of the new order. There were lively discussions upon religious tolerance, so unusual a word in Spain, and upon the instituting of trial by jury.

What was the behaviour of the tyrant during these discussions? He appeared as though he never for one moment failed to realize the insufficiency of this representation for the sanctioning so great a change. He always went on the principle *that acceptance by the nation* would replace the formalities which circumstances had made it impossible to fulfil.

That part of the constitution which concerned America was fairly liberal and calculated to maintain for some time the strides which that splendid part of the world had already taken towards independence. These articles of the constitution had been drawn up by a young Mexican canon, El Moral, a man having great wit, knowledge and love of his country. Generally speaking, whatever is good in Spain is excellent, but in no nation are enlightened minds in a smaller proportion. The more the body of a nation is behind the times, the more superiority and true greatness are to be found among the fifteen or twenty thousand patriots isolated in the midst of the riff-raff, and whose fame and fortunes echo throughout Europe. I never meet one of these noble victims without being amazed at the prodigious effort his mind must have made to raise itself above the thoughtlessness and false values[1] which had blunted the indomitable courage of the rest of the nation, to its own detriment. Men such as Auguste Arguelles, El Moral, Porlier and Llorente show Europe what Spain will become ten years after she has wrested from her kings a two-chamber government and put an end to the Inquisition.

Joseph and the Convention left Bayonne on July 7th. If what

[1] The action of false ethics which are the fruits of papism is very well developed in Vol. XVI of Sismondi's *History of Italy*.

had just happened had been judged solely by the retinue surrounding him, no one would have had any inkling of the amazing change which had just taken place. Joseph showed himself to the Spaniards amongst the same ministers and officers who had waited upon their former masters. Of all who had lived at the Bourbon court, only the king was changed. After that let it be said that the nobility are the support of kings! On the contrary, it is the nobility which make royalty odious.

Joseph arrived in a country of less than twelve million inhabitants, whose army had been carefully discredited, set aside or relegated to parts of the country remote from the monarchy.

For one hundred and fifty years the country had languished under the rule of a government that was hated and despised even more. State revenues which had been handled with the same ineptitude as everything else and squandered to boot, were in extreme disorder. And how was order to be restored to a country where work was considered a disgrace? In the more enlightened provinces, the people themselves had felt that it was imperative to change their king, and had looked to Archduke Charles.[1] How fortunate the Two Spains would have been if they had followed this idea! They would now have been enjoying the happiness which a wise and honest administration always confers, and with a foreign policy having nothing romantic about it. It is a far cry from the present state of Spain to that of subjects of the House of Austria!

Joseph made the same mistake as his brother. He did not despise the rabble sufficiently. He thought that to give the Spaniards equality and all the freedom they could conceive, would make them his friends. Far from this being the case, the Spaniards were piqued that the eighty thousand men sent to Spain were not picked troops; in this they saw a sign of contempt. From that moment all was lost. How, in fact, was one to handle a people who were ignorant, fanatical, abstemious in the midst of plenty and who took as much pride in their privations as other people took in their pleasures? The Spaniard is not

[1] The *Moniteur* of June 22nd, 1808.

covetous, he is even devoid of this source of activity. He saves without being miserly. He does not want to have gold as a miser does, but he doesn't know what to do with his wealth. He spends his days, lazy and sad, nursing his pride in the depths of a magnificent apartment. Blood, customs, speech, way of life and way of fighting, all these in Spain are Moorish. Were he Mohammedan, the Spaniard would be a complete Moor. He is consumed by the same fires, with a similar retiring disposition, a similar sobriety, a similar taste for meditation and silence. Ferocious yet generous at one and the same time; hospitable yet unrelenting; lazy yet tireless when on the move, burned by his sun and his superstitious beliefs, the Spaniard offers all the freakish characteristics of an irascible temperament carried to extreme. Moreover, like the Hebrews, he never goes outside his own house and from national prejudice remains aloof from contact with the other nations which surround it. A Spaniard's travels were limited to America where he found an even more degrading tyranny than that of the Peninsula. The Spaniard is not to be found in Europe. There are never any Spanish deserters, artists or traders. He is little known and for his part does not seek to know. The Spaniard possesses only one quality —he knows how to admire.

At Bayonne, people were in general much struck by the lack of knowledge which people attached to the Spanish court displayed with regard to the state of France. They had no knowledge of either men or events. They exhibited the curiosity of savages for the most famous generals of the French army.

The Spaniard, like the Turk whom he so strongly resembles in religion, does not leave his country to make war on other nations, but as soon as anyone sets foot in his country everyone is the enemy of the invader. The people do not think, as do the Germans, that it is the soldiers' business to defend them.

They have so much national pride; in Spain they are so patriotic that even the priests are patriots. Today half the generals who are fighting for freedom in America have risen from the priest class. That is yet another point of resemblance with the Turks.

The specific character of the priests is perhaps the main characteristic which divides Spain from the rest of Europe.

The clergy in Spain is *resident*. Moreover they are the only great landowners who live among the people. The others live in Madrid or in the provincial capitals. From this is derived the old saying which means to do something impossible: *To build castles in Spain*. This constant presence of the priest among the people, this continual restitution in the very place it was grown of the fruits of endeavour, is bound to give them an influence in which the absentee landlords, the nobles, can have no part. If the Spaniard listens to his priest as his superior in knowledge, he loves him as an equal in love of country. Priests detest liberal ideas. It is impossible to foresee how Spain will resolve this problem. It is a vicious circle perhaps destined to give future generations the useful and necessary spectacle of absolute monarchy.[1]

Spain had been afire for six months, yet Napoleon still believed that the blessings of a representative government would win him all hearts. He knew that of all European peoples, it was the one country that had carried admiration for his great achievements the farthest. Italians and Spaniards, having nothing frivolous in their character and being devoured by passion and suspicion, were the best judges of greatness in national leaders.

Had Bonaparte hanged the Prince of Peace, sent Ferdinand VII back to Spain with the Bayonne constitution; taken one of his nieces for wife, kept a garrison of eighty thousand men and made a clever man ambassador, he would have obtained from Spain all the ships and soldiers she could have provided. Who can assess the degree of adoration to which a nation might surrender when with them, adulatory praise becomes a paean and admiration turns to ecstasy?

There is no doubt that Napoleon was drawn by the example of Louis XIV. Once he had been aroused at Jena, he wanted to

[1] Tyranny tempered by an aristocracy of both nobles and priests, i.e., three powers conspiring against the useful and productive citizen, and plundering him at will.

do as much as that great king had done. He changed the king of precisely the one nation to which such a measure was unsuited. The ceaselessly renewed threats of M. de Talleyrand also played a great part in his decision.

At that very moment when Joseph was making his entry into Spain and when Napoleon was returning in triumph to Paris with his remorse and his false ideas, Spain had already risen. While the Council of Castile ordered a levy of three hundred thousand men, a great many parishes had already revolted of their own accord. There was not a village which did not possess its junta. Spain suddenly offered a spectacle similar to that of France when in 1793 she was covered with organized bodies of men deliberating upon the danger to which the country was exposed. At Seville, Badajoz and at Orvieto, the risings began at the news of the events which had taken place in Madrid on May 2nd. The whole of Asturias was in a state of insurrection upon learning of the change of dynasty. The mob began by making a terrible series of attacks upon all those whom it considered, in its rage, to be friends of France or lukewarm in the country's cause. The most important people were put to death. This resulted in a general *Terror* and in the need for all who governed to carry out unhesitatingly the will of the people. By means of the *Terror* Spain gained her armies.

As soon as an army had been defeated, it hanged its general. The Spaniards were a courageous and religious people, but not military-minded. On the contrary, it was customary for them to detest or to despise everything to do with soldiers. This was a complete contrast to Germany. They looked upon the war as a religious crusade against the French. A red ribbon bearing the inscription *Vincer o morir pro patria et pro Ferdinando VII* [*sic*][1] was the only military insignia worn by most of the soldiers.

The first battle which took place between these fanatics and the French, left twenty-seven thousand dead in the fields of the Rio Seco. Women threw themselves upon our wounded with

---

[1] To conquer or to die for Ferdinand VII.
Victory or death.(?)

terrible cries and fought each other to be allowed to finish them off by the most cruel tortures. They thrust knives and scissors into their eyes and then with savage joy gloated upon their blood and convulsions.[1]

Napoleon received news at Bordeaux of the battle of Baylen in which Castanos and Reding forced General Dupont to lay down his arms. It was his first setback and he was in despair. Neither Russia nor Waterloo affected in such a way this proud man.

'The stealing of holy vessels,' he cried in his rage, 'by an ill disciplined army is understandable; but to sign one's theft is not!'

Then a moment later:

'I know my Frenchmen. They should have been told *"sauve qui peut!"* and by the end of three weeks they would all have returned to me.'

He appealed to those present:

'Isn't there a law in any code to allow those abominable generals to be shot?'

[42]

NAPOLEON RETURNED TO PARIS, BUT SOON HAD TO LEAVE again for Spain. We will, as usual, leave aside the general history of the war which requires extensive detail. He reviewed troops at the gates of Madrid on several occasions. As was his custom, he found himself in the middle of a crowd of people and upon one occasion even, he found himself in the midst of a large column of Spanish prisoners. Ragged and sunburned, these defeated fanatics had horrible faces.

M. de Saint-Simon, a Spanish grandee and a former member of the Constituent Assembly, had fought in Madrid against the French. Napoleon pursued a definite policy in respect to Frenchmen who bore arms against their country. M. de Saint-Simon

[1] *Mémoirs* of Rocca, p. 190.

was arrested and condemned to death by a military commission. The Emperor could have had no feeling of hatred towards a man whom he did not know and who did not figure among those persons who were known to be dangerous. Policy alone had singled out the victim. M. de Saint-Simon had a daughter who eased his exile, and the troubles of his old age by her tender care. The danger to her father brought her to the feet of Napoleon. All preparations for carrying out the sentence had been made, but the devotion of this dutiful daughter prevailed over a set course of action which had seemed irrevocable, for it was based not on passion, but upon reason and upon recollections of Saint Jean d'Acre.

This noble act of clemency was made easier by the Major-General and by Generals Sebastiani and Laubardière. The whole army thought the Spanish war unjust. It had not yet been irritated by numerous acts of treachery.[1] During the retreat from Oporto in 1809, a crowded French hospital had been massacred in horrible circumstances. At Coïmbre, several thousand sick and wounded had also been despatched in a manner too atrocious to be related. Elsewhere seven hundred French prisoners were callously drowned in the Minho. There were hundreds of such incidents in which people whom one is still kind enough to admire were implicated. Little by little these atrocities irritated the French army, and it became cruel, although never as a matter of principle. All who were called rebels were shot or hanged.

Whilst engaged in his Spanish campaign, Napoleon heard that Austria, who had been arming for a long time, was about to attack him. It became necessary to entrust Spain or France and Italy to his lieutenants. He could not afford to hesitate. This was one mistake he could not avoid, and from that moment Spain was lost. The army, which ceased to be the Grande Armée, and was no longer blessed by the actual presence of the tyrant, grew daily more slack. From that moment, no matter

---

[1] 'It was one of our maxims that to mislead cleverly, without completely disguising the truth, a man as insincere as Napoleon, was an action which merited praise more than blame.' Escoïquiz, p. 124.

how brave the action, there ceased to be either reward or promotion for the army of Spain.

To make the position still more unbearable, the very obvious split between Joseph and Napoleon grew more and more embittered. In the beginning there had been two main reasons for this division; the way in which Napoleon had abandoned Joseph and the insolence of the marshals towards him; and secondly, Napoleon's new plans for Spain.

Joseph maintained that since he had been made a king, he should seem like one. To relegate him to the rear of the army was not the way to prepare him to become leader of the nation; and that the prouder the country the more it would wish her representative to be honoured. Louis XIV who understood vanity, would not have made such a mistake.

All the money brought back from Prussia, some one hundred millions, did not appear to be sufficient for the Spanish War. Accustomed to feeding one war with another, Napoleon could not get used to taking his own money into Spain. He wanted Joseph to pay for the war. Spain could have provided barely sufficient money in time of peace. It was supremely absurd to expect such a thing at a time when French troops were definitely masters solely of that territory which they had occupied militarily, and which they had drained dry.

But there was something else. No sooner had Napoleon set foot in Spain that he found beautiful what he saw and wished to have a part of it. Nothing was more opposed to the transactions of Bayonne. This quick-minded and intense genius, momentarily satisfied at the time of creation, constantly perceived fresh aspects of the matter. The new idea of each day supplanted that of the previous evening, and as he felt himself to be strong enough to overcome all obstacles, nothing was immutable to a mind before which the bounds of the possible receded as the horizon before the traveller. Napoleon has often been thought treacherous, when he was merely changeable. This was the frame of mind which made him, of all European princes, the least suited to a constitutional form of government.

At first, quite sincerely, he had yielded Spain to Joseph. Certainly at Bayonne he had not dreamed of appropriating a single one of his provinces. Upon his return from Benavente where he had pursued the English despite all the obstacles presented by snow, winter and mountains, he stopped at Vallodolid where he impatiently awaited the delegation from Madrid.

He sent for one of his courtiers who had travelled with the representatives. He was eager to set out for France. It was night and the weather was dreadful. Every minute or so he opened the window to see the state of the sky and to ascertain the possibility of setting forth. Turning towards the members of his Court, he asked question after question in his usual fashion, and inquired sharply what would happen at Madrid, what did the Spaniards want? He was told that they were discontented, whereupon he set out to prove that they were wrong and that discontent was an impossibility and that a nation always argued its own interests correctly, and that the Spaniards had to win the battle of tithes, equality, feudal rights and the lessening of the clerical Hydra. He was told that in the first place the Spaniard, knowing nothing of the state of Europe, was blind to its advantages, but that on the other hand he took pride in owing no one anything and that finally, as a race, the Spanish were like Sganarelle's wife who wanted to be beaten. Napoleon laughed and continued speaking vehemently while striding about the room.

'I did not know Spain; it is a much more beautiful country than I had thought. I made my brother a fine present. But you will see, the Spaniards will act stupidly, and the country will revert to me. Then I will divide it into five large viceroyalties.'

He was struck by the way Spain leaned towards an alliance with England. He did not count on the Napoleonic Spanish kings any more than upon the Bourbon Spanish kings. He felt that one as much as the other would take advantage of the first opportunity to gain their independence just as the kings of Holland and of Naples had tried to do.

He left Vallodolid the day after this extraordinary revelation.

After several hours' riding he covered the thirty leagues which separated that town from Burgos. Four days later he was in Paris. The speed at which he travelled, his aptitude for braving every kind of fatigue, were part of the magic of his being and everyone, even the most insignificant postillion, felt that he was a man above other men.[1]

[43]

LET US PAUSE FOR A MOMENT AND TURN TO THE PALACE OF the Tuileries where the fate of all Europe was decided.

The Spanish war marks both the decline of Napoleon's power and the period of decline of his genius. Prosperity had gradually altered and vitiated his character. He made the mistake of being too surprised by his success and of not sufficiently despising the kings, his colleagues. He drank great gulps of the poison of flattery. He believed that there was nothing personally impossible for him. He could no longer stand contradiction and soon the slightest remark appeared to him an impertinence and what was more, stupid. As a result of his bad choice (of men) he was used to seeing only those things succeed which he did himself. Very soon his ministers appeared to do no more than set down his ideas slavishly. Men of genuine ability drew away from him, or pretended to have ceased to think and laughed at him in secret.[2] It is impossible, in this age, for genuine ability not to be allied to fairly liberal ideas. Napoleon himself is an example of this, and it is considered the greatest crime of all.

[1] The summing up, full of facts, would only take one page (pp. 226 and suite, from Pradt), but it would chill. Keep it for some other place. Napoleon's character provides me with an excellent transition of ideas if not of words. July 10th, 1818.

[2] Count Réal, for example.

[44]

THE GOVERNMENT

THE EMPEROR HAD TWELVE MINISTERS[1] AND OVER FORTY States General councillors who sent him reports upon matters which he then returned to them. The ministers and the administrative heads of departments issued orders to the one hundred and twenty prefects. Four or five times every week each minister laid before Napoleon sixty or eighty draft decrees. Each of these drafts was amplified in the report which the minister read out to the Emperor. On matters of less importance the Emperor initialled his approval in the margin of the report.

The ministers left all signed decrees with the Duke of Bassano who retained the originals and sent the ministers certified true copies bearing his signature.

When the Emperor was with the army or travelling, the ministers, who did not accompany him, sent their portfolios to the Duke of Bassano, who then laid the decrees before His Majesty and read reports to him. This reveals the origin of the influence enjoyed by the Duke, who in the beginning was only a mere secretary who gradually managed to place his name at the end of those of the ministers in the Imperial Almanack, although he was never granted a ministry.

The all-powerful influence of the Duke of Bassano made itself felt over the ministers and prefects whom he frightened. No one had any influence over Napoleon on matters which he could understand. Therefore all decrees appertaining to organization, everything belonging to the domain of pure reason, if I may put it thus, proclaimed an outstanding genius. Whenever there were particulars that needed to be known, if the minister of the department involved was in agreement with the Secretary of State, Napoleon was misled during the preliminary exposé of the

[1] In 1810 there were MM. the Dukes of Massa, of Cadore, of Feltre, of Gaète, of Otranto, Montalivet, Mollien, Cessac, Decrès, Bigot-Préameneux and the Duke of Bassano. Later the Minister of Trade, Sussy.

matter, and pride or laziness caused him never to return to the subject.

As for decrees concerning personnel, Napoleon had adopted certain general rules based upon a supreme contempt for mankind. He seemed to think:

'As for people I do not know, I will be less likely to be misled by their uniform, which in my eyes places them in a certain class, than by the ministers.'

Each day saw him make the most absurd choice. Through seeking to inculcate respect in a witty and derisive people, he had suppressed conversation. His only means of knowing the people he employed was through outstanding success, or through his ministers' reports. Upon leaving Holland after a trip he had made there, he said with disarming naïveté:

'We are ill provided with prefects in this country!'

[45]

THIRTEEN AND A HALF YEARS OF SUCCESS TURNED ALEXander the Great into a kind of madman. Good fortune of exactly the same duration produced the same disorder in Napoleon. The only difference was that the Macedonian hero was lucky enough to die. What fame Napoleon the Conqueror would have left behind had a bullet killed him on the evening of the battle of Moskowa!

England and English writers could prevent the madness of the modern hero. He was unlucky in being obeyed too well in his rage against the English Press. Today this abhorred enemy is his only consolation.

In 1808, due to the changes which eight years of unhindered arrogance and *crownomania* had effected in Napoleon's genius, it transpired that out of his twelve ministers, at least eight were mediocre men having no other merit than that of killing themselves with work.

94

The Duke of Bassano, who enjoyed the greatest influence in non-military matters, and who was a pleasant and inoffensive man in the drawing-room, was, in the Government, of the most hopeless mediocrity. Not only was he devoid of any high aims, but he did not understand them. Everything that passed through his mind was diminished. He barely possessed the ability of a journalist; in which profession he had begun his career in Paris. Because of his position he had to be with the master night and day. A man of character would have taken offence at the fits of temper and at the Emperor's impatience, and however much of a courtier he might have been, his expression would have annoyed the monarch.

The Duke of Bassano chose all the prefects of France and expected no more of them than an ability to pluck a chicken without making it squawk. These unfortunate men who were filled with vanity, killed themselves with work and let their salaries be engulfed in an insane official display. Each morning upon opening their *Moniteur* they quaked for fear that they would find that they had been dismissed. One of their principal means of currying favour was to eradicate the last spark of public feeling which was known then, as now, under the name of Jacobinism.

[46]

THE GOVERNMENT (*continued*)

In 1811, a small rural community wished, for the sum of sixty francs, to use some bad paving stones which had been rejected by the engineer in charge of laying the main road. This required fourteen decisions by the prefect, the sub-prefect, the engineer and the minister. After incredible difficulties and extensive action the required authorization was finally received eleven months after the request had been made.

It then transpired that the bad paving stones had been used by workmen to fill up a hole in the road. A clerk, naturally ignorant of the matter, and kept at great expense in a corner of some ministry in Paris, two hundred leagues from the parish in question, had decided a matter which three representatives from the village could very well have settled in a couple of hours. Such an obvious act as this could not pass unnoticed, and it was one which occurred five hundred times a day.

But the main idea was to humble the citizen and above all to prevent him from discussing matters, which was an abominable habit contracted by the French in the days of Jacobinism.[1] Without such jealous precautions that other monster, to which I have already referred, abhorred by all the successive French governments who have exploited France, might have reappeared—and by this I mean the mind of the public.

It is clear from whence sprang the enormous amount of work which killed the Emperor's ministers. Paris wished to *digest* for the whole of France. All the affairs of France were to have been handled by people who, had there been eagles, could not have known about them.[2]

For the very life of a clerk tends necessarily to stupefy him. When he starts in an office, his primary occupation is to write a good hand and to know how to use the pounce-box. All the rest of his career is inclined to make him take the shadow for the substance. Should he succeed in acquiring an air of some importance, he has nothing further to desire. All his interests tend to make him favour the man who speaks without having seen. Both spectator and victim of the most sordid intrigues, the clerk combines the vices of a courtier with all the bad habits of the poverty in which he vegetates for two-thirds of his life. Such were the people to whom the Emperor had thrown France; yet he could despise them. The Emperor wanted France to be administered by clerks who earned one thousand two hundred francs a year. The clerk drew up the plan and the pride of the minister saw that it was passed.

[1] December 31st, 1817. The present government is as tyrannical as can be.

[2] Some foreigners may have pleasure in recalling the way in which a decree or law was put into practice. (Twenty lines explaining the functioning of the Administration.)

Something which depicts the period are the accounts of the paper manufacturers who supplied each minister. These are almost unbelievable. Almost as incredible, is the amount of useless, and therefore bad, work done by those unfortunate ministers and unhappy prefects. For instance, one of their most important jobs was to write out all reports in their own hand, as well as the different copies of each report for the various ministeries. And the more work they did of this kind, the more the ministry deteriorated. The only French ministry to function well was that of Mainz, whose prefect, Jean Debry, laughed openly at ministerial bureaucracy.

[47]

WHAT THEN WERE THE ATTAINMENTS OF THIS IMPERIAL administration so missed in France, as well as by Belgium, Piedmont, the Roman States and Florence?

There were general rules and vital laws dictated by the soundest motives. All those abuses which had accumulated in the administration of every country after two or three centuries of aristocratic rule and the shrewd use of power were completely uprooted. The general rules of French administration protected only two things: work and property. That was enough to ensure love for the régime. Furthermore, the ministerial decisions which came from Paris after a delay of six months, even though they were frequently absurd, due to an ignorance of the position, were always impartial. There is a certain country which shall remain nameless, where the most insignificant justice of the peace cannot issue a summons without committing a flagrant injustice to the advantage of the rich against the poor.[1] This régime was only interrupted by the setting up of French rule. Any man who wished to work could be certain of making his fortune. There were crowds of buyers for every article. Laws

[1] See *Consultations* by M. Dalpozzo, Italy, 1817.

97

and labour were honoured and made up for conscription and indirect taxation.

The Emperor's Council of State felt quite rightly that the only wise system was for each department to pay its own prefect, clergy, judges and for its departmental and municipal roads and then to send to Paris only what was needed for the sovereign, the armies, the ministers and finally, for general expenditure.[1]

This very simple system was the pet aversion of the ministers. The Emperor would no longer have been able to cheat the communes, which in France had been one of the sovereigns' great pleasures.[2] When the nation is no longer duped by fine phrases[3] this system will be accepted and then even the king will only be able to choose the prefects and mayors of large towns from among a certain number of candidates nominated by them.[4] And the smaller towns will nominate their own mayor for a period of one year. Until then there will be no true freedom and no genuine school for Members of Parliament. The finest elements of our legislative assemblies have been provincial administrators nominated by the people.

Instead of having matters dealt with by clerks, they will be handled by wealthy citizens to whom, as with hospital governors, the honour of the position will be sufficient payment. But all this frustrates a phrasemongering government and bureaucracy. In short, the deadly influence of a self-seeking city like Paris.[5]

[1] Lickspittles added to the Council of State: Chauvelin, Fréville and de Néville.

[2] People were amazed to see the Duke of Choiseul hold out for so long against Mme. Dubarry. At a time when he appeared to be most insecure, he found work with Louis XV and he asked him for orders relating to the five or six millions he had economized in the war department, pointing out that it would not be proper to pay them into the treasury. The King understood what that meant and told him: 'Speak to Bertin, give him three millions in kind, and I will make you a present of the remainder.' The King was not sure that a successor would offer him the same facilities.

[3] That is to say, when it shall have freedom of the Press.

[4] By people paying a hundred francs in taxes.

[5] All the petty men of letters who degrade literature and are used by the victorious party to defame the defeated one, as well as to extol its own insolence, live by office work. See the biographies of Michaud. (Villemain Roger, Auger.)

[48]

ON THE MINISTERS

WHILST ON THE THRONE NAPOLEON WAS UNFORTUNATE IN that he shared three weaknesses with Louis XIV.

He delighted in Court display to an almost childish degree. He appointed fools as ministers and, although he did not believe that he could shape them, as Louis XIV said of Chamillard, he at least thought that no matter how stupid their reports he would know how to sort out the root of the matter; in short, Louis XIV feared men of talent; Napoleon disliked them. He acted on the principle that in France there would never be a strong party other than the Jacobins.

He dismissed men like Lucien and Carnot: men of superior ability who possessed just the gifts in which he himself was lacking. He appeared to like or to endure Duroc, the Prince of Neuchâtel, the Duke of Massa, the Duke of Feltre, the Duke of Bassano, the Duke of Abrantès, Marmont, the Count of Montesquiou, Count of Cessac, etc., all of them perfectly honest and very worthy men among their contemporaries, but whom a shrewd public has always persisted in finding rather inept.

When the poisonous air of the Court had completely corrupted Napoleon and in magnifying his self-esteem to an unhealthy extent, he dismissed Talleyrand and Fouché and replaced them by the most narrow-minded of his sycophants (Savary and Bassano).

The Emperor reached the point of being able to deal with the most complicated matters in twenty minutes. He could be seen making the most incredible efforts of concentration, impossible to any other man, so as to understand a prolix and disordered report, in a word, one which had been written by a fool who did not understand the subject himself.

He said of the Count of C(essac), one of his ministers: 'He's an old woman'—and he kept him.

'I am not a Louis XV', he told his ministers at a council

meeting upon his return from one of his journeys. 'I do not change my ministers every six months.'

Then he went on from there to tell them all the faults with which the public reproached them. He thought he knew everything about everything and only needed secretaries to edit his thoughts. This might be the case with the leader of a republic, where public matters benefit from the intelligence of the most insignificant citizen, but not in the case of a despotic leader who cannot endure the existence of any corporate body, or of any regulations!

The Duke of Bassano's greatest success came from having guessed the Emperor's thoughts upon a certain matter, even before he had communicated them to him. Such was not the part played by Sully to Henri IV, nor would it be the rôle of a plain honest man towards a sovereign and above all towards a sovereign whose terrifying activity was such that he would settle by decree an expenditure of even fifty francs.

[49]

ON THE MINISTERS (*continued*)

FOR THE PAST TWO HUNDRED YEARS, A MINISTER IN FRANCE has been a man who signs four hundred dispatches a day and who gives dinners: a ridiculous existence.

Under Napoleon, these poor people killed themselves with work, but with work *without thought* and inevitably absurd. To be well received by the Emperor, one always had to solve the problem with which he was preoccupied at the moment of entering his presence. For instance: how much furniture is there in all my military hospitals? The minister who failed to answer promptly and as though he had thought of nothing else all day was abused, even though he possessed an intelligence equal to that of the Duke of Otranto.

When Napoleon learned that Crétet, the best Home Secretary he ever had was about to die of a fatal illness, he said: 'Just as it should be! A man whom I make a minister ought not to be able to make water after four years. It is an honour and an everlasting good fortune for his family.'

The unhappy ministers were completely dazed by this régime. The worthy Count Dejean was one day forced to ask for mercy. He had been calculating the war costs under the Emperor's dictation and was so *drunk* with figures and sums that he was forced to stop and to tell him that he could no longer follow.

Another minister fell asleep with his head upon his papers while the Emperor was talking to him, and he only woke up at the end of a quarter of an hour, still talking to His Majesty and replying to him—and he was one of the most brilliant.

The favour enjoyed by the ministers lasted for about a month or six weeks. When one of these unfortunate creatures saw that he no longer pleased the master, he would increase his output, grow yellow and become doubly ingratiating towards the Duke of Bassano. Then suddenly and quite unexpectedly they would return to favour. Their wives would be invited to join the Court circle and they became mad with joy. Such a life was killing, but it did not engender boredom. Months passed like days.

When the Emperor was pleased with them, he sent them an endowment of ten thousand francs a year. One day, having noticed a serious blunder which the Duke of Massa had caused him to make, he pushed him and his red gown upon a sofa and punched him several times. The next day, ashamed of his quick temper, he sent him sixty thousand francs. I have seen one of his finest generals (Count Curial) maintain that a blow from the Emperor was no dishonour, but merely a sign of dissatisfaction upon the part of the head of the French State. That is true, but one has to be very free from prejudice to realize it. Another time the Emperor struck the Prince of Neuchâtel with a pair of tongs.

The Duke of Otranto, who was the only man of genuinely superior intellectual ability among the ministers, excused himself from doing the enormous amount of pen work by means of which the other ministers sought to win the master's favour. Bénévent was only the *primus inter pares*, and his *pares*, ministers belonging to other Courts, were no better than idiots. He had nothing difficult to face. The Duke of Otranto had known how to save a government surrounded by enemies, and by exercising the most mistrustful of tyrannies, maintained a considerable pretence of liberty, and did not at all inconvenience the vast majority of Frenchmen. The Dukes of Massa and of Feltre were incapable of even such purely mechanical work. Annoyed by the ineptitude of the Duke of Feltre, the Emperor had his work examined by the Count of Lobau. The minister for the Navy and the Home Secretary, Counts Decrès and Montalivet, were clever men who did nothing but make stupid blunders. The former omitted to launch two hundred frigates armed as corsairs against English commerce, failed to train sailors quickly upon the Zuider Zee, as well as a thousand other absurdities. In the case of the latter, there were the guards of honour who were simply meant to remove five or six hundred chatterboxes who spoke ill of the government in the cafés, and who, in a most odious and unjust manner, caused grievous pain to thousands of families. But Count Montalivet longed for a dukedom—and yet he was a superior man!

In 1810 public opinion showed the Emperor its wish for the appointment of MM. Talleyrand, Fouché and Merlin to the Department of Justice; Soult to be Major-General; Carnot or Marshal Davoust to the War Department; Daru to Expenditure and War contracts; Chaptal to the Home Office; Mollien and Gaudin to the Ministry of Finance; Réal to be Secretary of State; Bérenger, Français, Montalivet, Thibeaudeau to the directorate; Le Voyer d'Argenson, Lezay-Marnezia, Count of Lobau, MM. Lafayette, Say, Merlin de Thionville to the Council of State. It is obvious that he followed this lead in part. Nevertheless, there were in his ministry four or five men who were so inferior that to have endured them indicates clearly his hatred of talent. It would have been much worse a few years later. Those who had acquired a genuine experience of affairs during the Revolution were becoming disgusted or were about to die, and the young people who would have replaced them, sought only to vie with each other in servility. To be well received by M. the Duke of Bassano was the supreme happiness. If one wished to be forever lost in the favour of this Duke, it was only necessary to display an ability to think. His favourites were people accused of being unable to read.

[50]

HOW THEN DID FRANCE FARE WITH MINISTERS WHO FOLlowed so absurd a course? France carried on by means of the excessive rivalry which Napoleon had inspired in all ranks of society. Fame was the real legislator of the French. Wherever the Emperor showed himself, and he travelled constantly over his vast empire, if real worth succeeded in breaking through the wall of ministers and chamberlains, it could be certain of an immense reward. The most insignificant chemist's apprentice working in his master's back-room was stirred by the thought that should he make some great discovery, he would receive the Cross of the Legion of Honour, and be made a Count.

The regulations governing the Legion of Honour were the only religion of the French. These rules were respected as much by the sovereign as by his subjects. Never since the ancient Romans' wreath of oak leaves had a public reward been distributed so wisely nor counted among its members so high a proportion of people of merit. All the men who had served the country usefully received the Cross. It had been somewhat lavishly bestowed in the beginning, but later only about a tenth of the members of the Order were devoid of merit.[1]

[1] Nowadays it is just the opposite. If anyone wants a list of all the most stupid, naïve and contemptible people in France, he has only to consult the list of all those who have received the Legion of Honour during the past three years.

[51]

ON THE COUNCIL OF STATE

MOST VITAL LAWS OTHER THAN THOSE RELATING TO PER-
sonnel were referred to the Council of State. It will be a long
time before any ruler will have such another Council. Napoleon
had inherited all the men of ability produced by the Revolution.
Exception was made only in the case of a very small number of
men who had been too prominent in a party. Through contempt for mankind, through indifference as to selection and
carelessness as to circumstances, he had buried in the Senate
several men whose integrity or whose abilities would have been
of use in the Council of State. Such were General Canclaux,
MM. Boissy d'Anglas, Count de Lapparent, Roederer, Garnier,
Chaptal, François de Neuchâteau, Sémonville. Count Sieyès,
Volney and Languinais had attracted too much attention by
their dangerous and liberal opinions. On the day the Concordat
was concluded, Volney had predicted to Napoleon all the annoyance the Pope would cause him.

With the exception of these men, the Council of State consisted of what was best under the circumstances. It was divided
into five sections.

The departments of Justice; The Home Office; Finance; War;
Navy.

If the Minister for War presented a decree on the organization of the *Invalides*, for instance, the Emperor would refer it
to the War Department, which asked nothing better than to
prove the minister at fault.

Decrees that were referred were debated in the department
concerned by six state councillors and four Masters of the
Court. There were seven or eight Commissioners of Audit. The
department drew up a draft that was printed parallel to that of
the minister. The printed sheet was distributed to the four
state councillors and both drafts were discussed during a meet-

ing presided over by the Emperor or the Vice-Chancellor, Cambacérès. Very often the decree was referred again to the department and then four or five different versions were printed and distributed before the Emperor could bring himself to sign it.

This was an excellent innovation which the Emperor introduced into despotic rule. It was a worthwhile power that any minister who knew his business would not fail to acquire from a ruler who was weak, or at least who only half understood the matter.

The meetings of the Council of State were occasions for the Emperor to show his brilliance. It was impossible to be more witty. In matters that were quite remote from his job as a general, during debates on the Civil Code, he was always astounding. His sagacity was marvellous, infinite, sparkling with wit, striking, bringing fresh light to bear upon every question or underlining relationships which had gone unnoticed: abounding in a lively and picturesque imagery, in spirited or, one might say, in *stinging* expressions that were all the more penetrating on account of the very incorrectness of his speech, which was always slightly odd, for he spoke neither French nor Italian accurately.

What was delightful was his frankness and his good nature. One day when they were discussing some business he had with the Pope, he remarked: 'It is easy enough to say that to you. But if the Pope said to me: "Tonight the Archangel Gabriel appeared to me and said so and so", I should have to believe him.'

Among the Council of State were hot-headed members from the south who grew animated and at times carried matters very far, and frequently they were not averse to advancing unsound arguments. Like Count Bérenger, for instance. The Emperor bore them no ill-will. On the contrary he liked to make them talk.

'Now then, Baron Louis, what have you to say on the matter?' The Emperor's common sense constantly altered the old absurd features of the official regulations with regard to

105

penalties. He was excellent when he criticized jurisprudence when arguing with old Count Treillard. Several of the wisest provisions in the Civil Code were his, especially on the subject of marriage.[1] The sittings of the Council were almost a picnic.

Cambacérès presided over the Council under him, as well as during his absence. Cambacérès displayed superior ability and great sense. His summing up was admirable. He soothed wounded self-esteem and while calling to order every error of a speaker striving to be clever, he yet knew how to draw from him whatever light he might be able to cast upon a matter. (It is to the Council of State) that is due the admirable French administration: an administration which despite severed relationships, Belgium, Italy and the Rhineland provinces still regret.

The Emperor wished neither to encourage dangerous republican virtues among the citizenry nor to found great schools such as the Polytechnic, for judges and administrators. How far the idea was from his mind; he never visited the Polytechnic, which is a large military establishment whose success had surpassed the hopes of the philosophers who had founded it, and which had already filled the army with excellent majors and captains.

Apart from these two deteriorating conditions French administration was something that will never be improved upon. Everything about it was firm, reasonable and devoid of foolishness. It was said that there was too much scribbling and bureaucracy. Those who raised this objection forgot that the Emperor did not want, under any circumstance, any unwieldy left-overs from the republics. The despot said to his subjects: 'Cross your arms, my prefects will take care of everything for you. As the price of such sweet repose, I only ask for your children and money.' Since the majority of the generals had grown rich through their pilfering, it was necessary, by means of inspections and counter-inspections, to render such knavery impossible.

[1] See Locré's *Discussions* although Locré is very uninteresting.

106

Never again will a tyrant have administrators such as Count François de Nantes for indirect taxes, which brought in one hundred and eighty millions, and Count Montalivet for the Department of Communications which cost between thirty and forty millions. Or like Count Duchâtel, the ruthless director of the Crown Lands who, although he owed his position to his wife, was nevertheless excellent. Count Lavalette, the Postmaster-General, might jeopardize half France, as well as the Duke of Otranto, but in this matter he only did what was essential. This was considerable commendation since it was due to integrity of character. Count Daru, the most upright of men, had an exceptional talent for feeding an army. Count de Sussy was a good Director of Customs and Excise. The Emperor was the mortal enemy of trade, which rendered people independent. Count Sussy was a thousand times too much of a courtier to defend trade against the master's aversion for it. Merlin, at the Supreme Court of Appeal, and Pelet de la Lozère as Chief of Police were also admirable. In the Emperor's hands the Press became a means of vilifying or of degrading any man who had incurred his displeasure. But, although violent and unrestrained in his fits of temper, he was neither cruel nor vindictive. He offended many more than he punished, observed one of the men who had had most cause to feel the weight of his anger. Count Réal was a man who was possibly superior to any of the others; one of those men who should be of the company surrounding a despot.

The best element in the Council of State were former liberals, called Jacobins, who had sold their conscience to the Emperor for a title and twenty-five thousand francs a year. The majority of these gifted people were on bended knees before a Collar of the Legion of Honour[1] and were almost as base as Counts Laplace and Fontanes.

The Council was admirable until the Emperor surrounded himself with a Court—that is until 1810. Then the ministers openly aspired to become what they had been under Louis XIV.

[1] Count Francais, for instance.

It was gullible and therefore ridiculous to oppose openly the draft decrees of a minister. A few years more and it would have been shocking, in a departmental report, to have held a different opinion to that of the minister. All frankness of style was abolished. The Emperor called several men to the Council of State who, far from being children of the Revolution, had, in the prefectures, only acquired the habit of an exaggerated obsequiousness and of blind respect for the ministers.[1] The supreme merit of a prefect lay in imitating the conduct of a brigadier-general in conquered territory. Count Regnault-de-Saint-Jean-d'Angely, the most corrupt of men, gradually became the despot of the Council of State. The lack of honest people could be felt. Not because they let themselves be bought (there was hardly any doubtful integrity other than that of Regnault), but there was a lack of those rather surly and upright people whom nothing will prevent from telling ministers an unpleasant truth.

The Caffarelli brothers were of this type, but every day this quality grew more old-fashioned and absurd. There soon remained only Counts Defermon and Andréossy who, carried away by their teasing disposition, dared to refuse to bow before the minister's draft decrees. The latter made it a matter of personal vanity to see that all the draft decrees issued by their offices were passed, and gradually state councillors were replaced by clerks, and the draft decrees were no longer discussed except by the Emperor, at the moment of signing them.

Finally, at the fall of the Empire, this Council of State which had created the Civil Code and French administration had become almost insignificant, and those who foresaw the ministers' plans, spoke of its destruction.

Towards the end of his reign, the Emperor often held a Council of Ministers or a Cabinet meeting which some senators and state councillors were invited to attend. There they discussed matters that could not well be confided to fifty people. That was the real Council of State. These meetings would have been all that was necessary if it had been possible for some

[1] Molé, Chauvelin, Fréville and Néville.

independence of thought to have been admitted there. I do not mean in respect to the master, but in respect to the influential ministers. Who would have dared to say in front of Count Montalivet that the internal administration was declining day by day, that every day one of the benefits gained by the Revolution was lost?

As a result of the suppression of conversation, the Emperor occasionally felt the need, especially at night, to pour out his thoughts. He went hunting for ideas. It was then that ideas came to him which meditation would not have brought him. While satisfying this inclination, he would sound the person with whom he spoke, or it would be better to say that the politician remembered what the philosopher had heard the previous evening. Therefore, one day at two o'clock in the morning, he said to one of his officers: 'What will happen to France when I am gone?'

'Sire, your successor, who quite understandably will be afraid of being overwhelmed by the weight of your fame, will seek to underline the faults in your administration. A deficit will be declared for the fifteen or twenty millions that you do not wish your war department to pay to the unhappy merchants of Lodève, etc. . . .'

The Emperor discussed the matter like the most outspoken and unaffected of philosophers, and one might also add, like a most profound and agreeable one. Two months later, a complaint by some contractors was being discussed at a Cabinet meeting. The officer with whom Napoleon had discussed the future only a month before was speaking:

'Oh, as for you,' interrupted the Emperor, 'I know you to be a friend to the contractors.'

Nothing was farther from the truth.

⌈ 52 ⌉

ON THE COURT

In 1785 there was 'society', that is to say that people who were indifferent to one another assembled together in a drawing-room and succeeded in obtaining if not any great enjoyment, at least a very delicate and constantly renewed pleasure. Indeed *social pleasures* grew to be so indispensable that they succeeded in smothering the sensual pleasures which belong to man's intimate nature and which are a part of the very essence of great emotions and of the higher virtues. Everything strong and sublime could no longer be found in the hearts of the French. Love alone gave rise to a few rare exceptions.[1] But, since great emotions are only to be met with at widely spaced intervals, whereas drawing-room pleasures are ever present, French society possessed a charm induced by the stringent rules which governed speech and manners.

Without anyone realizing it this extreme politeness had completely vitiated the energy of the wealthy classes of the nation. There remained that type of individual courage which has its roots in excessive vanity, and which would seem to be aroused and constantly increased within the heart by good manners.

Such was France when the lovely Marie-Antoinette, seeking to procure for herself the pleasures due to a pretty woman, turned the Court into Society. People were no longer well received at Versailles merely because they were a Duke and Peer, but because Madame de Polignac was pleased to find them agreeable.[2] It so happened that neither the King nor the Queen was very intelligent. Furthermore, the King lacked character and since he was accessible to anyone who offered advice,[3] he did not know how to put complete trust in a Prime Minister[4] nor yet

[1] We are not concerned with nine-tenths of society who are neither polite nor influential.
[2] *Mémoires* of Bézenval.
[3] Even to Pezay who told him when to use his handkerchief.
[4] By upholding the wise Turgot.

110

how to ride upon the bandwagon of public opinion. For some time it had not been worth while to attend Court, but M. Necker's first reforms directed against friends of the Queen[1] made this fact obvious to all. From then on the Court ceased to exist.[2]

The Revolution was started by the enthusiasm of noble minds from every class. The right wing of the Constituent Assembly set up an ill-timed resistance and energy was needed to overcome it. This meant calling into the fray all young men of the middle classes who had not grown degenerate through an excess of good manners.[3] All the European kings formed a league against Jacobinism. It was then that we had the sublime uprising of 1792 when surplus energy was required as well as young men from an even lower class; an uprising in which very young men found themselves at the head of everything.[4] Our greatest generals came out of the ranks to assume command, as though it were some game, of armies of 100,000 men.[5] At this moment, the greatest in the annals of France, good manners were proscribed by law. Anyone who was polite became quite rightly suspect to a people surrounded by traitors and treachery, and it is obvious that the people were not far wrong in having envisaged a counter-revolution.[6]

But it is not through laws or a movement of enthusiasm that a race or an individual can renounce an old habit. Upon the collapse of the Terror, the French were seen to return frantically to social pleasures.[7] It was in Barras's drawing-room that Bonaparte glimpsed for the first time the delicate and entrancing delights procured by an accomplished society. But like the slave who appeared in the market-place at Athens loaded with

[1] M. de Coigny.
[2] All this will no doubt be admirably described in the posthumous work of Mme. de Staël who by her talents was called upon to write the *Esprit des lois* of Society.
[3] MM. Barnave, Mounier, Thibeaudeau, Bérenger, Boissy d'Anglas, Merlin, etc.
[4] Danton, Saint-Just, Collot d'Herbois, d'Eglantine and all the very energetic rabble of the Convention and of the Jacobins.
[5] General Hoche, son of a fruiterer. Moreau, a law student.
[6] For information on the conspiracies of the period, see the *Biographie des vivants*, by Michaud.
[7] The balls for the victims. Mme. Tallien's salon.

gold pieces, yet without any copper change, his mind was too fine, his imagination too inflamed and too quick for him ever to have known success in a salon. Moreover, he made his first appearance there at the age of twenty-six, with a character that was already formed and inflexible.

Upon Napoleon's return from Egypt, the Court of the Tuileries was, at first, like an evening round the camp fires. Behaviour there was frank and natural and devoid of wit. Mme. Bonaparte alone and almost furtively tried to encourage the display of feminine arts and graces. The society of her daughter Hortense and her own influence gradually softened the iron character of the First Consul. He admired the politeness and decorum of M. de Talleyrand, who owed to his manners an amazing freedom.[1]

Bonaparte realized two things which were that if he wished to be King, a Court was required to win over the weak French people on whom the word Court exerts an all-powerful influence. He saw that he was in the hands of the military and that a conspiracy of praetorian guards could cast him down from the throne to death.[2] A Court circle composed of palace prefects, chamberlains, equerries, ministers and ladies of the Court would inspire respect in the generals of the Guards, who were also French and therefore had an innate respect for the word Court.

But the tyrant was mistrustful. His minister Fouché had spies even among the marshals. The Emperor possessed five different police forces who controlled one another.[3] A single word expressing less than adoration, I will not go so far as to say for the tyrant but for tyranny, was sufficient to damn one forever.

He had aroused everyone's ambition to the highest pitch. With a king who had been an artillery lieutenant, and with marshals who had begun life as village fiddlers or fencing

[1] The anecdote of the cherries. 'Your Majesty owns the most beautiful cherries of his Empire.'
[2] Remember the admirable conspiracy of General Mallet, October 1812.
[3] Those of the Minister; of the Chief Inspector of Gendarmeri of the Prefect of Police; of the Postmaster-General, and finally the Secret Police which was in direct contact with the Emperor.

masters[1] there was no Commissioner of Audit who did not aspire to be a minister[2]; no second-lieutenant who did not aspire to the sword of High Constable. Finally, the Emperor wanted to assemble his Court within two years. There was nothing that rendered a people more servile[3]: and once that had been achieved, he wanted to institute principles of conduct. The police intervened in a most uncouth manner in the misadventure of one unhappy lady of the Court.[4] In short, the Court consisted of generals and young men who had never known good manners, which went out in 1789.[5]

It did not take much more to prevent the rebirth of social intercourse. There was no more Society. Everyone shut himself up within his own household and it became an era of conjugal virtue.

One of my friends who is a general, wished to give a dinner for twenty people. He went to Véry's restaurant in the Palais Royal. Having listened to his order, Véry then said to him: 'No doubt you are aware, General, that I am obliged to notify the police of your dinner, so that they may send someone to it.' The general was much surprised and even more annoyed. That evening, finding the Duke of Otranto at a Council meeting at the Emperor's he said to him:

'*Parbleu*, it is going too far when I cannot give a dinner for twenty guests, without letting in one of your people!' The minister apologized, but did not waive the required condition. The general grew indignant. Finally Fouché said, as though

[1] Victor, Duke of Belluno, fiddler at Valence. Augereau, a fencing master at Naples under the protection of Ambassador Talleyrand, who gave him 25 louis to go and make his fortune in France.

[2] After the example of M. Molé.

[3] Between 1808 and 1810, he had said to a rich Paris jeweller who had three daughters: 'General N . . . will marry the elder of your three daughters to whom you will give 50,000 écus.' The distracted father, who had access to the Tuileries, went to beg him for mercy: Napoleon repeated the same words, adding: 'General N . . . will pay his court tomorrow and will marry the girl the next day.' They are now a very happy couple.

[4] Mme. Rapp.

[5] For instance, Minister Roland going to see the King without any buckles on his shoes.

struck by an idea: 'But let us see your list of guests.' The general handed it to him. The minister had barely read a third of the names than he began to smile and, handing back the list he said: 'There is no need for you to invite anyone unknown.' The twenty guests were all people of importance!

What the monarch most disliked after public witticisms, was worldly wit. In a passion he banned the *Intrigante*, a comedy written by an author in the pay of authority,[1] yet in which jokes were made about his chamberlains and in which fun was made of the ladies of the Court who, under Louis XV, had created colonels. Such humour which was so very foreign to him, shocked him deeply. Someone had dared to make fun of a Court!

Among a witty people who would laughingly sacrifice a fortune for the pleasure of making a good joke, each month saw the birth of some new and malicious jest. This upset Napoleon. At times impudence was carried as far as a song, then he would be bad-tempered for a week and maltreat his chiefs of police.[2] What envenomed his despair was the fact that he was very sensitive to the pleasure of having a Court.

His second marriage revealed a fresh weakness of character. He was tickled by the idea that he, an artillery lieutenant, had succeeded in marrying the grand-daughter of Maria-Theresa. The vain pomp and ceremony of a Court appeared to give him as much pleasure as though he had been born a prince. He attained the height of folly by forgetting his main qualification, that of being a child of the Revolution. Frederick, Duke of Würtemberg and an authentic king, said to him at one of those congresses which Napoleon held in Paris so as to justify, in the

---

[1] Etienne. (Note by Colomb.)

[2] The song, by Michaud:

> This hero is worth his weight in gold,
> In France none doubts this;
> But he would be worth e'en more
> Were he worth all he costs us (bis).

The song by that contemptible Martainville caused him to be drenched with water at Charenton by special influence of the Duke of Rovico.

eyes of the French, his title of Emperor: 'I see no historic names at your Court. I would have all these people hanged or else I would relegate them to my ante-room.' This is possibly the only major piece of advice that Napoloen ever followed, and he followed it with a respect that was, in itself, quite ridiculous. Immediately the hundred leading French families went to beg M. de Talleyrand to force them to reappear at Court. In surprise, the Emperor said: 'I wanted to have the young of the nobility in my armies, and I was unable to find any.'

Napoleon reminded the great families that their nobility had nothing to do with him: for they had forgotten this. But he was obliged, as he has since admitted, to touch upon this sensitive point with extreme caution.

'Because every time I touched that cord, people's minds shied like a horse whose bridle is pulled too tight.' He offended against the one passion—vanity—of the French people. As long as he had only offended against liberty, everyone had admired him.

When, in his youth, Napoleon had been poor and completely devoted to serious matters, he had nevertheless been very far from indifferent to women. His extremely thin appearance, his smallness and his poverty were not likely to give him confidence or to bring him many successes. It had required courage in small doses. It would not surprise me to think of him as having been shy with women. He feared their ridicule and this man to whom fear was unknown, revenged himself upon them in his heyday by constantly and crudely expressing a fine contempt for them to which he would not have referred had it been true. Before his elevation to power, he wrote to his friend Director Rey, about a passionate love affair in which Lucien was entangled:

'Women are like muddy sticks: one cannot pick them up without being soiled.' By means of this inelegant image he sought to point out the errors of conduct to which they led; it was a prophecy. If he hated women it was because he had a supreme fear of the ridicule which they dispensed. Finding himself at dinner with Mme. de Staël, whom it would have been so easy to have won over, he said coarsely that he only liked women who attended to their children. He wanted to have, and it is said that with the help of his valet, Constant,[1] he did have almost all the women at his Court. One of them, a bride, remarked to her neighbour upon her second appearance at the Tuileries. 'Good heavens, I can't imagine what the Emperor wants of me. I have received an invitation to be in the private apartments at eight o'clock.' The next day the ladies inquired whether she had seen the Emperor, and she blushed exceedingly.

Seated at a small table, his sword by his side, the Emperor would be busy signing decrees. The lady would enter the room. Without moving he would tell her to get into bed. Shortly after, carrying a candle he would show her out and would then return to reading his decrees, correcting and signing them. The essential part of the interview had lasted no more than three minutes. Frequently his mameluke was behind a screen.[2] He had sixteen such interviews with Mlle. George, and at one or them he gave her a fistful of banknotes: there were ninety-six in all. This had been arranged by the valet Constant. Sometimes Napoleon would ask the lady to take off her shift and then, without troubling to move, he would send her away.

Such conduct on the part of the Emperor drove the women of Paris to despair. To send them away after two minutes so as to sign his decrees and frequently without even removing his sword, seemed to them frightful, as it amounted to making them eat dirt. He would have been better liked than Louis XIV if only he had pretended to have a mistress and had thrown her a couple of prefectures, twenty masters' certificates and ten vacancies for Commissioners of Audit to distribute. What would it have mattered to him? Was he not aware that upon formal introductions from his ministers he himself occasionally appointed their mistresses' protégés?

[1] Faithfully translated from the works of Goldsmith.
[2] This mameluke and Constant received an income of 20,000 francs from their master, but they were ungrateful and didn't even follow him to Elba. They are now enjoying their fortune in Paris.

He was misled by the appearance of weakness. It was the same as his weakness for religion. Should a politician mistake for weakness that which would have gained him the support of all the women? Then there would not have been so many white handkerchiefs to greet the return of the Bourbons.

But he hated women and fear knows no reason. The wife of one of his ministers committed a single indiscretion. Napoleon had the savage cruelty to tell her husband. The poor man, who worshipped his wife, fainted. 'And you, Maret, did you imagine that you were not a cuckold? Last Wednesday your wife slept with General Pir.'

There was nothing more vapid and one might say more stupid than the questions which he would put to women at the balls given by the city of Paris. In a sombre and bored tone of voice this delightful man would ask: 'What is your name? What does your husband do? How many children have you?' When he wished to fill to overflowing the measure of distinction, he would pass on to the fourth question: 'How many sons have you?'

For the ladies of the Court, the supreme favour was to be invited to join the Empress's entourage. At the time of the fire at Prince Schwartzenberg's he wished to reward several ladies who had behaved with distinction during the great danger which had suddenly appeared in the midst of the pleasures of a ball.

The Court circle began at eight o'clock at Saint-Cloud. Besides the Emperor and Empress it was composed of seven ladies and of MM. de Ségur, de Montesquiou and de Beauharnais. In a fairly small room, the seven ladies, in full Court dress, stood in a row against one wall. The Emperor, seated beside a small table, looked at some papers. At the end of a quarter of an hour of profound silence he rose and said: 'I am tired of working. Tell Costaz to come in; I will go over the plans for the Palace.'

Baron Costaz, the most puffy of men, entered carrying the plans under one arm. The Emperor had him explain to him the amount to be spent the following year upon Fontainebleau, which he wanted to finish within five years. He first read the proposed plan, breaking off from time to time to make remarks to M. Costaz. He did not find the calculations correct which the latter had made for filling in a pond they wanted to silt up. He then began to calculate in the margins of the report. He forgot to sprinkle sand over his figures, he scratched them out and covered himself with ink: he made mistakes. M. Costaz reminded him of the figures from memory. During all this, he had turned to the Empress two or three times and said: 'Well! have these ladies no conversation?' Then, very softly, a few words would be whispered on the subject of the universal talents of His Majesty, and an even deeper silence would fall once more. Three-quarters of an hour would pass in this fashion, and then the Emperor would once again turn around and say: 'But these ladies aren't talking—my dear, send for a game of lotto.' A bell would be rung and the game brought, while the Emperor went on with his calculations. He had sent for a fresh piece of paper and had begun all his calculations afresh. From time to time he was carried away by his own quickness. He made mistakes and grew annoyed. In difficult moments such as these, the man who was taking the lotto numbers out of a bag lowered his voice even more until it became no more than a mere movement of the lips. The ladies around him were barely able to guess the numbers he called. Finally it would strike ten; the dreary game of lotto was broken off and the evening at an end. Formerly people would have returned to Paris to boast that they had been at Saint-Cloud. But nowadays that is no longer sufficient; a Court is a very difficult thing to create.

The Emperor was singularly fortunate in that his good star caused him to chance upon someone who was peculiarly well suited to be the leader of a Court. This was Count de Narbonne, doubly a son of Louis XV.[1] Napoleon wanted to make him a

[1] The one who, when he was Minister of War, declared war on everyone at the start of the Revolution, and made his round of official military visits followed by Mme. de Staël.

gentleman-in-waiting to the Empress Marie-Louise. The Princess had the unexpected courage to oppose him.

'I have nothing with which to reproach the present gentleman-in-waiting, Count Beauharnais.'

'But he is so stupid.'

'Your Majesty might have thought of that before he appointed him. It is not seemly that he should leave without any reason, and above all that he should leave without me.'

The Emperor had not the wit to say to Count de Narbonne: 'Here are five million francs to spend in a year, with absolute power over the department of trivialities. Form an agreeable Court for me.' The mere presence of this delightful man would have been sufficient.

At the very least, the Emperor should have asked him to write amusing repartees for him. The Minister of Police longed for a phrase that he could praise to the skies. Far from doing any such thing, the Emperor appeared to consider it a matter of duty to compose his Court from among the most boring faces in the world. The Prince of Neuchâtel, who was a great horseman, was of no use in society, where he always appeared to be in a surly temper. M. de Ségur had been pleasant,[1] which was certainly more than could be said for MM. de Montesquiou, de Beauharnais, and de Turenne, for even for that poor man Duroc who, it was believed thee'd and thou'd the Emperor in private. Nothing could be more dull than the rabble of equerries and chamberlains. There were never more than a dozen of these to be seen in the palace ante-rooms, and then they were always the same faces, and among them there was nothing capable of relieving the boredom of the Court. I should not be surprised if the Emperor, to whom an entertaining mind was completely

[1] The Master had confided to him the composition of the etiquette to be observed at the Imperial Palace; a volume of 306 pages, published by Galand in 1808; as well as the abuse of Philosophy at the Institute on the day the Count de Tracy was received. It was amusing to see what high-sounding phrases the great Chamberlain used to rebuke poor, unfortunate Philosophy. In 1817, having no official position, the great Chamberlain became a liberal.*

*True, but (in English in the text) it had best be cut.

119

foreign, felt an aversion for such people who are indispensable
to Court life if it is to compete with that of the city. All the men
attached to the Court at Saint-Cloud were the most honest
people in the world. There was no meanness of soul to be found
at this Court which was eaten up with ambition; there was only
an overwhelming boredom. The Emperor was never anything
more than a genius. It was not in his nature to be amusing.
Plays either bored him or else he conceived such a passion for
one that to listen to it and to enjoy it became his all-absorbing
preoccupation. He would therefore be wild with delight upon
hearing Crescentini sing Romeo and Juliet and the aria *Ombra
adorata, aspetta*, and only emerge from his transport of joy to
send him an iron crown. The same thing would occasionally
happen when Talma was playing Corneille, or when Napoleon
was reading Ossian, or when he caused some old folk-dances to
be played at one of the parties given by either Princess Pauline
or Queen Hortense, in which he would whole-heartedly take
part. But he never possessed the composure that is required to be
agreeable. In a word, Napoleon was unable to be another Louis XV.

Since the Arts had made immense strides during the Revolution and since the collapse of bogus good manners, and since the
Emperor possessed very good taste and desired that all the
monies he paid out in salaries or in rewards should be spent, the
fêtes given at the Tuileries or at Saint-Cloud were enchanting.
They only lacked people capable of being amused. There was no
way of procuring ease and abandon, as people were too eaten up
with ambition and with the fear or hope of success. Under
Louis XV, a man's career was a foregone conclusion. It took
something out of the ordinary to make any changes in it. The
pretty Duchess of Bassano gave balls which were very much
enjoyed. The first two were agreeable—the third one divine.
The Emperor saw her at Saint-Cloud and told her that it was
unfitting for a minister to give a ball in dress clothes: and
ended by reducing her to tears.

It was obvious that among leaders of the Court, Society
would survive only if an everlasting state of constraint, vacuity

and reserve were maintained. The most bitter enemies were brought face to face. There was no private social life.

The baseness of the courtiers was not masked by pleasant words as under Louis XV.

Count Laplace, Chancellor of the Senate, reproached his wife for not taking sufficient trouble with her dress when she went to see the Empress. The poor woman who was very concerned with her appearance, bought a lovely dress which was unfortunately so charming that it took the Emperor's eye. He thereupon came up to her as soon as she had entered the room and in front of two hundred people said:

'Well, you *have* got yourself up, Mme. Laplace. But you are old! You should leave such clothes to younger women. They are no longer suitable for women of your age.'

Unfortunately, Mme. Laplace, who was known for her claims to beauty, was just at that most difficult time when it takes a pretty woman to admit that she is no longer young. The poor woman returned home in despair. Her friends among the senators, without seeking to remind her of these cruel words, were prepared, so shocking had the incident been, to find the master in the wrong, should she refer to it again. Then M. Laplace arrived and said: 'But Madame, what possessed you to choose a gown fit for a young girl! You absolutely refuse to grow old . . . and yet you are no longer young . . . the Emperor was quite right.' For an entire week no one could talk of anything except this typical courtier's remark. And one must admit that it was not gracious, and a credit neither to master nor servant.

[53]

ON THE ARMY

THE MEN PICKED BY NAPOLEON DURING HIS CONSTANT REviews after consulting soldiers as well as regimental public opinion were excellent, whereas those of the Prince of Neuchâtel were very poor.[1] To possess wits was in itself sufficient reason for being passed over; and even more so the slightest display of warmly enthusiastic patriotism.

Nevertheless it is evident that stupidity was indispensable only to officers of the Guards who, above all else should not be of a type likely to be susceptible to proclamations. It was only blind instruments of the will of Mohammed that were required.

Public opinion had named the Duke of Dalmatia or the Count de Lobau for the post of Chief-of-Staff. The Prince de Neuchâtel would have been more pleased than either of these to have had the appointment. He was weary with the strain of his position, and for days on end he would put his feet up on his desk and lolling back in his chair would whistle in answer to any request for instructions which might be made.

What was wonderful in the French army were the non-commissioned officers and men. As it cost a great deal to buy oneself out of conscription all the children of the petty bourgeoisie were in the ranks, and, thanks to State schools, they had read *Emile* and *Caesar's Commentaries*. There was not a second-lieutenant who did not firmly believe that by fighting well and failing to stop a bullet, he would one day become a field-

[1] Opposite this passage Stendhal had written these words: 'The Prince of Neuchâtel possessed all the moral virtues of an honest man, but it is permitted to cast doubts upon his abilities.'

Then, at the end of the MS. among pieces to be inserted later, was this judgement: 'The Prince of Neuchâtel, brought up at Versailles in the lower ranks of the Court, and the son of a man who, through geography, had succeeded in pleasing Louis XV never possessed the Republican enthusiasm which had fired the majority of our generals in their youth. He was an exceedingly complete product of the training of the Court of Louis XVI; an extremely honest man with a hatred for everything having either grandeur or generosity. He was the one man in the army least able to understand the wholly Roman character of Napoleon. Therefore, although he pleased the tyrant by his Court manners, he constantly offended the great man by his ancien régime sentiments. When he became Chief-of-Staff and a Prince, he pondered for some time upon the form of address he should use at the end of his letters. It became known that his sycophants carried out extensive research at the Bibliothèque Nationale, but none of their suggestions appeared to suit him. In the end he decided that he would conclude his letters without any form of address, merely signing them with his princely name of Alexander. Moreover, he possessed all the private virtues. He was only mediocre as a prince and general. Although somewhat brusque in manner, he was socially pleasant.' (Note by French editor.)

marshal. This happy illusion was retained until the rank of brigadier. It then became apparent, in the ante-room of the Prince Vice-High Constable that, unless an heroic action were performed immediately under the eyes of the great man, one's only hope lay in intrigue. The Chief-of-Staff surrounded himself by a kind of court so as to keep at a distance those marshals whom he felt were worth more than he. As Chief-of-Staff promotion in all armies outside France lay with the Prince of Neuchâtel. The Ministry of War only dealt with the advancement of the military employed inside France, where it was customary for promotion to follow solely upon the sound of gun shots. One day, at a Council of Cabinet Ministers, the worthy General Dejean, the Home Secretary, General Gassendi and several others met to request the Emperor to promote an artillery captain who had rendered the greatest service inside the country. The Minister of War recalled that in the course of the past four years His Majesty had struck this officer's name off the promotion lists no less than three times. They had all ceased to employ the official tone of voice, so as to beseech the Emperor.

'No, *messieurs*, I will never agree to the promotion of an officer who, for ten years, has not been under fire. But it is sufficiently well known that I have a Minister of War who obtains my signature by fraud.' The next day, the Emperor signed the decree gazetting this brave man a major in the Infantry, without reading it.

When he was with the army after a victory or after a mere advance carried out by a division, the Emperor would always review the troops. After he had walked along the ranks with the colonel of the regiment, and had spoken to all the men who had distinguished themselves, he would order the drums to be rolled while the officers grouped themselves around him. Then, if a major in command of a group of artillery had been killed he would ask in a loud voice: 'Who is the bravest captain?' There, in the heat of enthusiasm for victory and for the great man, hearts were sincere, and the replies honest. Should the bravest captain not have sufficient means to be an artillery major, he would promote him in the Legion of Honour and, returning to the question, he would ask:

'After so and so, who is the bravest captain?' The Prince of Neuchâtel then made a pencilled note of all promotions and the Emperor would at once pass on to the next regiment, while the commander-in-chief of the regiment he had just left confirmed the officers in their new ranks.

At moments such as these I have often seen the men weeping tears of affection for the great man. At the very moment of triumph the great Victor would send off lists containing the names of thirty or forty people to be decorated or to receive promotion. These lists usually bore his signature scribbled in pencil on the field of battle and which are therefore still in existence, preserved in the National Archives, and one day after the death of Napoleon, they will constitute a touching memorial for history. Upon rare occasions when a general had not had the brains to propose a list, the Emperor would have the bad taste to say:

'I grant two officers medals and ten medals for legionaries to such and such a regiment.' Such manners ill accord with fame.

When he visited hospitals, amputated and dying officers with the red medal of the Legion of Honour pinned to their wooden bedsteads would risk asking for the iron crown; but he did not always grant it, as it was the highest distinction of all.

The cult of Glory; the unexpected; an absolute enthusiasm for glory which meant that a quarter of an hour afterwards one let oneself be killed with pleasure, all combined to set intrigue at naught.

[54]

ON THE ARMY (*continued*)

MOREOVER, THE SPIRIT OF THE ARMY VARIED; FIERCE Republican and heroic at Marengo, it grew more and more selfish and monarchical. Gradually as uniforms became embroidered and loaded with medals, they covered hearts that were less generous. All generals (like General Desaix, for instance) who fought with enthusiasm were either removed or were kept idle. The schemers triumphed and the Emperor dared not punish their guilt. A colonel who fled or who managed to slip into a ditch every time his regiment was under fire, was made a brigadier and sent to the rear. The army was so selfish and so corrupt during the Russian campaign that it was almost upon the point of telling its general to go to hell.[1] Moreover, the follies of the Chief-of-Staff,[2] the insolence of the Guards regiments who enjoyed every privilege[3] and who for long had not been in battle, since they had become the perpetual reserve troops of the army, alienated many hearts from Napoleon. Gallantry was not at all diminished (it is impossible for soldiers of a vain-glorious nation not to let themselves be killed a thousand times over, so as to be the bravest of all), but the soldier, having no discipline, lacked prudence and ruined his physical strength without which qualities courage alone must fail.

One of my friends who is a colonel, told me on our way to Russia that in the past three years he had seen 36,000 men pass through his regiment. Each year there was less training, less discipline, less patience and less implicit obedience. A few marshals like Davoust and Suchet still held their army corps together, but the majority appeared to be at the head of disorder. The army no longer knew how to co-ordinate itself. It was due to this that the Cossacks, who were only wretched, ill-armed peasants, were destined to win a victory over the bravest army in the world. I have seen twenty-two Cossacks, the eldest of whom was only twenty years of age, with only two years service to his credit, throw into disorder a column of five hundred Frenchmen; that was during the Saxon campaign of 1813.[4]

---

[1] To go to hell does not seem quite right to me. Possibly I have forgotten the facts.

[2] Careful, replace *follies* by errors.

[3] Order of the day at Moscow about October 10th, for non-commissioned officers and men who did not feel strong enough to walk 10 leagues a day.

[4] Near Gorlitz, twenty paces from the house in which the Duke of Frioul had just died.

The Cossacks could have achieved nothing against the Republican army of Marengo; but since such an army will never be seen again, the king who rules the Cossacks, rules the world.[1]

[55]

WHEN THE EMPEROR UNDERTOOK THE WAR WITH RUSSIA, she had been popular in France since the weakness of Louis XV had permitted the division of Poland. Since the population of France had remained stationary among sovereign states who were all increasing theirs, she was obliged, sooner or later to resume her first place or else be reduced to a secondary category. All the kings felt the need for a successful war with Russia, so as to deprive her of the means of invading Southern Europe. Therefore was it not natural to take advantage of a time when a great military figure occupied the French throne and offset the country's tremendous disadvantages?

Besides such general reasons, the war of 1812 was the natural outcome of the Treaty of Tilsit, and Napoleon had right on his side. Russia, who had promised to ban English goods, was unable to fulfil her undertaking. Napoleon took up arms to punish her for violating a treaty to which she owed her very existence, which Napoleon could have destroyed at Tilsit. Thenceforth kings will know that a defeated ruler should never be spared.

[56[2]]

IT IS A LITTLE OVER A CENTURY SINCE THE GROUND ON which the loveliest of capitals, Saint Petersburg, is built, was no

[1] See the trip to Vienna of M. Cadet-Gassicourt in 1809. His is no treacherous pen.
This chapter is the connecting link between the chapter on the Council of State and the Court with the course of events.
[2] Copying M. Royer, we have taken this chapter out of the *Correspondence*, where it had been inserted by Colomb at the date when, no doubt, it had been written: August 18th, 1818. (Note of French editor.)

more than a barren marsh, and all the surrounding country lay under the domination of Sweden, at that time an ally and neighbour of Poland; a kingdom of seventeen million inhabitants. Since Peter the Great, Russia had always believed that by 1819 she would be the mistress of Europe, if she had the courage to desire it and that America would then be the only country capable of withstanding her. That, it may be said, amounted to looking very far ahead indeed. See how far we have travelled since the Peace of Tilsit in 1807. At the time that that peace treaty was concluded, all the military predicted that if ever there were a contest between France and Russia, the outcome of the battle would be decisive for one or other of the two countries—and it was not France who had the better chance. Her apparent superiority hung by a man's life. Russia's strength was increasing rapidly and was due to force of circumstances. Moreover, the Russians could not be attacked. There is only one defence against the Russians and that is a very hot climate. In three years they lost through illness in their Moldavian army, thirty-six generals and one hundred and twenty thousand men.

Napoleon was therefore quite right to have tried to stop Russia while France had a great man for absolute ruler. The King of Rome, born to the throne, would probably not have been a great man and even less of a despotic ruler. The Senate and the Legislative Body would have had, sooner or later, to have taken vigorous action, and certainly the influence of the French Emperor would have collapsed in Italy and in Germany upon the death of Napoleon. Nothing could be wiser than the projected war with Russia and, since the primary right of every individual is self-preservation, there could have been nothing more right.

Poland through her intercourse with Stockholm and Constantinople was a formidable bulwark for Southern Europe. Austria and Prussia had had the stupidity and Louis XV the folly to lend a hand in destroying this unique pledge of their future security. Napoleon had to try and re-establish this bulwark.

Perhaps history will blame him for having made peace at

Tilsit. If he had been able to do anything else, it would have been a big mistake. Not only was the Russian army weak and exhausted, but Alexander had realized what was lacking in its organization.

'I gained time,' he said after Tilsit, 'and never was delay put to better advantage. In five years the Russian army, already so brave, became almost as well organized as the French army, with the added advantage that one French soldier costs his country as much as four Russian soldiers.'

The whole of the Russian nobility was concerned either closely or remotely in the commercial interests involved in peace with England. When their sovereign opposed them they arranged his disappearance. On the Russian side, therefore, war with France was equally essential.

Since the war was essential, was Napoleon right to have undertaken it in 1812? He was afraid that Russia might make peace with Turkey, that English influence in Saint Petersburg would increase and finally that his reverses in Spain, which he was no longer able to conceal, might encourage his allies to recover their independence.

Several of Napoleon's advisers pointed out to him that it might be advisable to send 80,000 men to Spain so as to finish off matters there before *getting into a fix in the north* (those were the words they used). Napoleon replied that it would be much wiser to leave the English army in Spain: 'If I run them out of the Peninsula, they will come and land at Königsberg.'

On June 24th, 1812, Napoleon crossed the Nieman at Kovno, at the head of an army of 400,000. This was Southern Europe seeking to crush its future master. Two political mishaps marked the start of this campaign. The Turks, as stupid as they were honest, made peace with Russia: and Sweden, wisely assessing her own position, came out against France.

After the battle of the Moskova, Napoleon was able to let his army go into winter quarters and to restore Poland, the real aim of the war, which he had achieved almost without firing a shot. Through vanity and so as to wipe out his misfortunes in

Spain, he wished to take Moscow. There would have been no drawbacks to this impudence if he had only stayed twenty days in the Kremlin, but his ever mediocre political genius cost him his army.

Having reached Moscow on September 14th, 1812, Napoleon should have left there on October 1st. He allowed himself to be deceived by the hope of concluding a peace. If he had evacuated the city, the heroic burning of Moscow[1] would have become ridiculous.

Towards October 15th, although the weather was superb and there were still only three degrees of frost, everyone realized that it was more than time to make a decision. Three alternatives presented themselves:

To retire upon Smolensk, hold the line of the Borysthenes (Dnieper) and reorganize Poland.

To spend the winter at Moscow, living on what stores could be found in the cellars and by sacrificing the horses, which could have been salted down and then to advance upon Saint Petersburg in the spring.

Thirdly and lastly, since the Russian army which had suffered greatly on September 7th,[2] was farther off to the left, to have executed a flank sortie to the right and to have reached Saint Petersburg which was defenceless and had no wish to burn itself. In such a position peace would have been a certainty. If the French army had been as vigorous as it had been in 1794, the third alternative would have been chosen. But the mere suggestion of such a thing would have caused our rich marshals and elegant brigadier-generals to shudder as they left the Court.

One of the drawbacks to this plan was that it meant remaining cut off from France for five months, and the Mallet conspiracy showed to what kind of people the Government had been confided in the absence of a jealous master. If the Senate or the Legislative Body had been worth anything the leader's absence need not have been fatal. During the march from Moscow to

[1] The burning of Moscow began during the night of September 14th–15th.
[2] At Borodino.

Saint Petersburg, the whole of the left flank of the army would have been disengaged and for a whole month Napoleon could have sent a daily courier and thereby have governed France. With Marie-Louise as Regent, Cambacérès as head of civil affairs and the Prince of Eckmühl at the head of military affairs everything would have functioned properly. Ney or Gouvion Saint-Cyr at Mitau and Riga could have sent one or two couriers a month. Napoleon himself could have gone to Paris, since a Russian army inside Russia is of necessity immovable for three months. Man can only survive such terrible cold by spending ten hours of each day by the side of a stove. The Russian army reached Vilna as decimated as was our own.

Of the three alternatives the worst was chosen. Yet, what was worse, it was carried out in a most absurd fashion, because Napoleon was no longer the general he had been while with the army in Egypt.

The discipline of the army had suffered as a result of the plundering which it had been absolutely necessary to allow at Moscow since no rations were issued to the troops. With the French character there is nothing so dangerous as a retreat. And it is during danger that discipline, which means strength, is required.

It became necessary to inform the army by means of a detailed proclamation, that it was going to Smolensk and that it therefore had to cover ninety-three leagues in twenty-five days. Each soldier was to be given two sheepskins, one horse-shoe and twenty calkins, as well as four oil-cakes. Each regiment could have only six carriages and a hundred pack-horses. Finally, for twenty-five days any insubordination would be punished by death. Every colonel and general supported by two officers would have the right to order any insubordinate or marauding soldier to be instantly shot.

The army had to be prepared for departure by a week of good food with issues of a little wine and sugar. Stomachs had suffered greatly during the march from Vitebsk to Moscow for, as a result of lack of foresight, they had found how to run out of bread in Poland.

Finally, all these precautions having been taken, it was necessary to reach Smolensk by avoiding as far as possible the route which had been laid waste on the way to Moscow, and along which the Russians had burned all the cities: Mojaisk, Giatsk, Viasma, Dorogobough, etc.

On all these points action contradicted prudence, Napoleon. who no longer dared have a soldier shot, was careful not to mention discipline. Upon its way back from Moscow to Smolensk, the army was preceded by thirty thousand deserters who claimed to be ill, yet who appeared to be very well indeed for the first ten days. These men wasted and burned everything they did not use. The soldier who was loyal to his flag looked like a fool. And since that is the one thing which the French dislike above all else, there were soon only men of heroic character or nincompoops under arms.

Soldiers frequently told me during the retreat, though I have difficulty in believing it, as I never saw it, that in an order of the day issued at Moscow towards the October 10th, the Prince of Neuchâtel had authorized all soldiers who did not feel well enough to do ten leagues a day, to go on in advance. The men immediately got worked up and began to calculate the number of marching days it would take to reach Paris.

[57]

NAPOLEON USED TO SAY: 'IF I SUCCEED IN RUSSIA, I SHALL be master of the whole world.' He allowed himself to be defeated not by men, but by his own pride and by the climate;[1] and Europe took up a new attitude. The minor princes ceased to tremble, the great kings were no longer irresolute and all looked to Russia which had become the centre of an invincible opposition.

[1] It should not be thought that winter was early, on the contrary, at Moscow, the weather was as fine as could be desired. When we left on October 19th there were three degrees of frost and a superb sun.

The English ministers had not calculated upon this good fortune; those very ministers who only possessed influence because they took advantage of a freedom which they hated. Russia will advance from the position in which they have placed her, and will recommence the achievements of Napoleon in a much more invincible way, because it will be more than just a life interest. We shall see the Russians in India.

No one in Russia was as yet surprised by a despotic form of government. It was confused with religion and since it was exercised by the kindest and most pleasant of men, only a few travelled philosophers were shocked by it. Russian soldiers were indifferent to proclamations or decoration, and only moved by the order of Saint Nicholas. General Masséna once related in my presence how a Russian soldier, upon seeing a comrade fall, is persuaded that he will resuscitate in his homeland, and bends down to ask him to convey news of him to his mother. Like the Romans,[1] Russia has superstitious soldiers commanded by officers who are as civilized as we are.[2]

Napoleon clearly felt that the course of centuries had just been changed when at Warsaw he said:

'It is only a step from the sublime to the ridiculous.' He then added: 'Success will make the Russians daring. I will fight two or three battles against them between the Elbe and the Oder and, within six months, I shall again be upon the banks of the Nieman.'

The battles of Lützen and of Wurtchen were the final effort of a great people whose spirit was destroyed by a disheartening tyranny. At Lützen one hundred and fifty thousand men from units that had never previously been under fire, fought for the first time. These youngsters remained aghast at the sight of the carnage. Victory brought no cheerfulness to the army. An armistice had become necessary.

[1] Montesquieu: *Religion des Romains*.
[2] See the pamphlet by Sir Robert Wilson, 1817. In 1810 and 1811, the Russian Minister of War had all Napoleon's military orders translated and put into practice.

[58]

On May 26th, 1813, Napoleon was at Breslau. There he was rash in three ways; he relied too much upon his army; too much upon the stupidity of foreign governments; too much upon the friendship of kings. He had created and saved Bavaria; the Austrian Emperor was his father-in-law and a natural enemy of Russia. He was the dupe of both these claims.

He should have taken advantage of the moment of respite to exhaust the resources of the conquered countries, and ten days before the armistice he should have taken up a position at Frankfort-on-Main. Then the whole Russian campaign would have been saved, that is to say in so far as it concerned France, and the Empire would not have been broken up. But Napoleon no longer possessed any influence beyond the Elbe, except in as much as he was the greatest prince in Europe.

The Silesian expedition was inopportunely confided to Marshal MacDonald, known only for his reverses; the Battle of Dresden; the foresaking of the body of Marshal Saint-Cyr; the Battles of Leipzig; the Battle of Hanau, all that was a mass of colossal mistakes[1] such as could only have been committed by the greatest military figure to have appeared since Caesar.[2]

As for the peace terms that were constantly being offered to him, time will show if there was anything sincere[3] in it all. For my part, I believe in the sincerity of the governments of the period, because I believe in their fear. Moreover, the type of mind needed to acquire something is not the same as the type of mind that is used to preserve something. If, on the day following the conclusion of the peace treaty at Tilsit, Napoleon's

[1] Napoleon's rage after Dupont's capitulation. The Council meeting at which M. de Saint-Vallier was present. Napoleon's rage shook the windows of the Tuileries. He took great strides about the room.

[2] There is one man who may be an excellent military historian of these great events. That is the rescuer of Count Lavalette, General Robert Wilson. I think that on all military matters, Napoleon's Memoirs will be perfectly correct.

[3] See the Prague negotiations which were published in the *Moniteur* of the first days of August 1813, and in the *Edinburgh Annual Register*.

whole genius had been transformed into plain common sense, he would still be master of the better part of Europe.

But you, reader, you would not possess half the liberal ideas which now excite you; instead you would be intriguing for the post of chamberlain or of petty army officer, and as a consequence of proving yourself one of the Emperor's henchmen, you would have striven to rise a step in rank.

[59]

AT DRESDEN AFTER THE BATTLE OF AUGUST 26TH, Napoleon seems to have been the victim of a false point of honour; he did not want to withdraw. Familiarity with the throne had increased the man's pride and lessened his common sense, which in his early years had been so remarkable

This total eclipse of common sense is even more noticeable in his acts of home administration. In the course of this same year he caused his despicable Senate to quash the sentence which the Brussels Court of Appeal had pronounced in the matter of the town dues of Antwerp and upon the findings of a jury. He was thus at one and the same time both legislator, prosecutor and judge; all out of pique through having discovered rogues who had been more shrewd than his own regulations.

Another senatus-consultum clearly reveals the despot who had fallen a prey to madness. This act of the Senate was in the first place absurd in its departure from the established ways known as the Constitutions of the Empire; it declared that peace could never be concluded with England until she had returned Guadaloupe, which she had just given to Sweden. The members of the Senate, most of whom were considered, prior to their election, to be among the most outstanding men in France, vied with each other in ignominy once they were assembled within the Luxembourg Palace. A courageous opposition tried to put them to shame, but in vain. They replied: 'The age of

Louis XIV has returned, and we have no wish to ruin ourselves and our families for ever.' Since the debates were held in secret, the opposition knew only the perils of opposition and none of its glories, and a doubly grateful posterity should remember the names of Tracy, Grégoire, Lanjuinais, Cabanis, Boissy D'Anglas, Lenoir La Roche, Colaud, Cholet, Volney and a few others. They are famous men who even today are still among the opposition and who are still abused by the same sycophants who have merely changed their master.[1]

Napoleon ordered all his prefects to abuse Bernadotte, Prince of Sweden, in hundreds of speeches that were doubly ridiculous since Bernadotte had taken Swedish nationality upon leaving France.[2]

Meanwhile, Wellington, triumphing through force of circumstances over a less clever general than he, was nearing Bayonne. Holland was in revolt. The forty-four gendarmes who happened to be the only garrison in Amsterdam on the day of one of the calmest revolts in history, were unable to prevent that country from detaching itself from France. The most impregnable fortified towns were occupied as though they were villages. Inside the country the Emperor had left not a man, not a bullet or, what was more important, not a single capable head. The most that could be done was to keep Berg-op-Zoom and shortly afterwards the French garrison, having captured the English Army Corps that beseiged it, showed the world that:

disjecti membra poetae.

After the Dutch rising appeared the Frankfort Declaration which promised Belgium and the left bank of the Rhine to France. But what was there to guarantee such a promise? What was to prevent the allies from re-opening hostilities six months after the peace? Posterity will remember the good faith displayed by the allies after the surrender of Dresden and of Dantzig.

[1] *To see: Stael's* Considerations *for the names.*
[2] See the *Moniteur*, as is only right. The most base signatories of these addresses were men who, two years later, were to display a most absurd and bloodthirsty extremism. See the speech of M. S(éguier).

[60¹]

ALL THE PARTS OF THE EMPIRE SEEMED TO TOPPLE ONE upon another. Despite these frightful disasters, Napoleon still had a thousand means of arresting the course of his decline. But he was no longer the Napoleon of Egypt and of Marengo. Obstinacy had replaced talent. He could not bring himself to abandon his vast plans which for so long had been considered, both by his ministers and himself, to be absolutely infallible. In time of need he found himself surrounded solely by courtiers. This man whom feudalists such as the English and Mme de Staël have described as being Machiavellism incarnate: like one of the incarnations of evil;² was twice the dupe of his own heart. First, when he believed that the friendship which he had inspired in Alexander would make that prince do the impossible; and second, when he thought that because upon four occasions he had spared the House of Austria instead of destroying it, that it would not abandon him in his misfortune. He said that the House of Austria would see the bad position in which it stood in regard to Russia. Bavaria, which he had set up in 1805 and saved in 1809, deserted him and tried to give him his *coup-de-grâce* at Hanau. If the Bavarian general had had twenty trenches dug across the road, he would have succeeded. Napoleon possessed the defect of all *parvenus*; that of having too great an opinion of the class into which he had risen.

While on the road from Hanau to Paris, Napoleon had not the slightest inkling of his danger. He remembered the exalted spirit of 1792; but he was no longer the First Consul of a Republic. To have overthrown the Consul it would have been necessary to have defeated thirty million men. In fourteen years of administration, he had degraded men's hearts and had replaced a somewhat gullible Republican enthusiasm by a monarchic egoism. Thus the monarchy was remodelled and the monarch

¹ This chapter is rather disconnected.
² The very words of Mme de Staël: in *Leviathan*, I think, Vol. 2.

could be changed without any real revolution having taken place. What did it matter to the people concerned ?[1]

On the other hand, for fourteen years we had had kings who were frightened to death. If they thought of the illustrious House of Bourbon at all, it was to see in what sort of state they might find themselves from one day to the next. After the Battle of Leipzig intrigues were quelled for a time and true merit was able to approach the Court.[2] Thus patriotism and enthusiasm were in the Allied camp together with the Land-sturm and the Landwehr, and they contained men of merit. Napoleon had paralysed enthusiasm and instead of having Carnot for Minister of War as at Marengo, he had the Duke of Feltre.

[61]

HAVING REACHED FRANKFORT, THE ALLIES SEEMED SUR-prised at their success. They had at first discussed the idea of penetrating into Italy : French soil frightened them and they had the retreat from the Champagne constantly in mind. Finally, they dared to cross the Rhine (January 4th, 1814).

Napoleon had been for some time in Paris. His main object was, I believe, to gain reassurance against the fear with which the French people inspired him. He issued decrees merely to procure uniforms, rifles and boots, as though morale were of no importance. He aimed at disentangling himself from such an embarrassing situation without surrendering any of his majesty. For the first time in his life, he seemed small. His poor sub-editors whom he had called ministers, were afraid of a blow in in the legs from the fire-tongs and hardly dared to breathe.

The Emperor formed the National Guard. If France were to have a second Terror, which is highly possible if the priests and nobles are allowed to do what they like, the National Guard

---

[1] If there was a revolution, it was due solely to the follies of the ministers of 1815.
[2] MM. Stein, Gneisenau.

would help to make it less horrible than the first one. All the semi-riff-raff will be found enlisted in it and small shopkeepers who will fear plunder will intimidate the worst of the rabble. If France chanced to be thrown into a different series of events, the National Guard will also serve to uphold the aristocracy of wealth. It might make certain stages of the inevitable fight between privilege and rights somewhat less bloody. For the National Guard to be completely reassuring in this respect, every year the soldiers should be allowed to elect their own officers up to the rank of captain and to submit candidates for the higher grades. The proportion of taxes to be paid by each rank should be fixed.

In January 1814 the most vital people in Europe were, as a nation, nothing better than a corpse. It was in vain that some thirty Senators had been given the mission of trying to arouse those same French people who had been so terrible under Carnot. All of us felt certain that by showing them the red Phrygian bonnet they would have acquired in less than six weeks a more ruddy complexion from the blood of all the foreigners who had dared to sully the sacred soil of Liberty. But the Master cried to us: 'One more retreat and one people's community the less.' Had he regained the Empire, woe betide he who had failed to hear this command! It was during that time that Napoleon must have felt the weight of his nobility. What results were we to expect from proclamations that were addressed to the hearts of the people, and which began with feudal titles? Pictures of heroism. Fierce love of country.

One outstanding characteristic of this period (January 1814) was the tone of the ministers' correspondence, above all that of Minister M(ontalivet).[1]

If a Senator informed him that he had not five hundred rifles in good condition, the minister merely replied: 'Arm the schools: French youth has heard the voice of its Emperor', and

[1] Stendhal had first written the name in full. He then crossed it out leaving only the initial and wrote in the margin: 'Out of consideration for the misfortunes of the Home Secretary, Montalivet.' (Note by French editor.)

similar phrases which the most impudent journalist would have considered too exaggerated for a proclamation. It was so excessive that several times we asked ourselves :

'Is he committing treason ?'

In a final fit of temper and thoughtlessness which ultimately overthrew France, and which posterity will find difficulty in believing, so closely allied was it to folly : at a time when it was imperative for the Emperor to court his people, he started a quarrel with the Legislative Body. He accused the most honest people in the world of having sold themselves to foreign powers, and he wound up the session of the Legislative Body.

That was what despotism did to one of the greatest geniuses who ever lived.

[62]

IN PARIS, ON THE MORNING OF JANUARY 24TH, NAPOLEON showed himself to be a great tragic actor. A dark veil had begun to descend upon the fortunes of France. The confidence of the chief of state was the people's confidence. As soon as fear appeared, all eyes were turned towards him.

He was reviewing the National Guard of Paris in that courtyard of the Carrousel where all Europe had come to watch the Guards manœuvre. He stood in front of that Triumphal Arch adorned with those mighty trophies which he was so soon to lose. It seemed as though the grandeur of the setting had influenced him and he was moved by it. He had the officers of the National Guard informed that they were to go up to the Salle des Maréchaux. For a moment they all thought he was going to suggest that they should leave Paris and march upon the enemy. Suddenly he came out of the Galerie de la Paix and appeared before them with his son in his arms. He presented the young King of Rome to them and said:

'I place this child, the hope of France, in your care. As for me I go forth to battle, my only thought the salvation of the country.' Instantly tears appeared in the eyes of everyone present at the sight of the Man of Destiny speaking from his heart. I shall remember this heart-rending scene all my life.[1] My tears angered me. Each moment reason told me: 'In the days of men like Carnot and Danton the Government, if confronted with so urgent a peril, would have done better than merely try to touch hearts that were weak and lacking in courage.'

In fact, the same people who on January 24th wept at the Tuileries, on March 31st waved white handkerchiefs from every window and appeared to be drunk with joy when Emperor Alexander rode along the boulevards. It should be pointed out that on March 31st the question of the illustrious House of Bourbon had not yet arisen, and that Parisians were overjoyed merely because they found themselves conquered.

[63]

UNDER SIMILAR CIRCUMSTANCES, THE CONVENTION HAD decreed that on such a day the soil of Liberty would be purged of the presence of the enemy, and upon the day appointed the armies carried out the order.

On January 25th, 1814, the day of the Emperor's departure, a matter which concerned the whole of France seemed to have become the business of one man. The grandiloquence to which this man gave expression in his speeches and which, in his halcyon days had won him all the faint-hearted, was now the reason why everyone secretly enjoyed seeing him humiliated.

Many people longed for the taking of Paris merely as a spectacle. When I rejected this remark with horror, one of these people said quite rightly: 'Paris is a capital that no longer suits France. Seven hundred thousand egoists who are the most

[1]January 24th, 1814, Beyle was not in Paris, but at Grenoble with Count de Saint-Vallier. (Note by Colomb.)

pusillanimous and characterless people born in France find
themselves through force of custom the representatives of
France in all revolutions. You may rest assured that fear of
losing their mahogany furniture will always make them commit
every act of cowardice that is suggested to them. It is not their
fault. An excessive meanness has completely atrophied their
souls in all except purely personal matters. The capital of
France should be a city capable of defence situated beyond the
Loire, near Saumur.'

[64]

THE CONGRESS OF CHATILLON BEGAN ON FEBRUARY 4TH
and ended March 18th. One great power was opposed to Napoleon's downfall. With the support of this great power he could
in all security have made peace. But he would have considered
himself dishonoured if he had accepted a France diminished by
so much as one single village from what she had been when he
had received her on the 18th Brumaire. That was indubitably
the mistake of a great spirit; the misconception of a hero! And
in it lay the whole secret of his conduct. Other princes proved
themselves to be free from any such futile delicacy.[1]

[65]

THE DEFENCES WHICH NAPOLEON UNDERTOOK AROUND
Paris were romantic, but none the less they were upon the point
of succeeding. French armies were dispersed over immense
distances; at Dantzig, at Hamburg, Corfu and in Italy.
The west and the Vendée were in a ferment. Close at hand
this conflagration was nothing, but from a distance it aroused
fear. The south flared up and assassinations were feared.

[1] In a footnote some pointless abuse from the Staël.

Bordeaux had declared itself in favour of the king who was ultimately to give us a constitutional form of government. The north deliberated with that calm which had distinguished it throughout the whole course of the Revolution. The east, inspired by the noblest sentiments, only asked for the arms with which to cleanse the soil of France.

Deaf to the voice of reason which advised him to throw himself into the arms of Austria, Napoleon appeared to be solely preoccupied by his admirable campaign against the Allies. With seventy thousand men he resisted an army of two hundred thousand and defeated it repeatedly. The army fought desperately, and in all fairness for honour's sake. The army was far from foreseeing the fate in store for it. It is said that the generals did not do so well as the soldiers and ordinary officers; for they were rich. The allied armies also displayed courage. They were ten to one. The Landwehr and the Tugendbund[1] had introduced a patriotic enthusiasm into their ranks, but, however, since their generals were not self-made men but princes nominated by birth, the fortunes of battle were variable. Napoleon, so mediocre as a monarch, as a general frequently recovered the genius of his early years. He spent two months dashing from the Seine to the Marne and from the Marne to the Seine.

What posterity will perhaps most admire in the military career of this great man, are the battles of Champaubert, Montmirail, Vauchamp, Mormant, Montereau, Craonne, Rheims, Arcis-sur-Aube and Saint-Dizier. His genius was consumed in a feeling similar to that of a brave man about to draw his sword against a fencing master. Moreover, he was mad: he refused the offer of the Army of Italy, one hundred thousand strong, which Prince Eugène offered him through the intermediary of M. de Tonnerre. A few days later a shell fell ten feet from his horse and instead of moving aside, he stepped over it. The shell burst four feet from him without wounding him. I am inclined to think that he was putting his fate to the test.

Near Laon on March 13th, the Emperor was joined while

---

[1] A society founded in part by the witty Dr. Arndt.

under fire by Prince Bernadotte's doctor. Again peace proposals were made to him. That was the last voice to be used by
destiny.

[66]

NAPOLEON HAD LONG CHERISHED THE IDEA OF PUSHING A
small advance force into Alsace. It was a question of reinforcing
his army with all the eastern garrisons and of then falling upon
the rear of the allied army. Decimated by sickness, fearing an
open revolt of the Lorraine and Alsatian peasants who had, on all
sides, already begun to murder soldiers cut off from their units;
and lastly, upon the verge of an almost total lack of supplies,
war material and of food, the enemy army was about to retreat.

The Emperor's plan would have succeeded had Paris possessed the courage of Madrid. This daring plan would still have
succeeded had the basest treachery not taken a hand in it. A
foreigner upon whom Napoleon had showered undeserved
favours; the Duke of Dal(matia), sent a messenger to Emperor Alexander. This messenger informed the Emperor that
Napoleon was marching towards Lorraine with the aim of wip-
ing out the allied army during its retreat and had left Paris
defenceless. That word changed everything. When the messenger arrived the Allies had, for the past twenty-four hours,
already begun to fall back upon the Rhine and Dijon. The
Russian generals had said that it was high time to put an end to
such a romantic campaign and to go and capture those places
which had been unwisely left in the rear.

After the messenger had been received, Emperor Alexander
wished to advance forthwith, but the Austrian Commander-in-
Chief opposed this with the full weight of his authority, even to
the point of forcing Alexander to say that he would assume full
responsibility.[1] What reader is not struck by a sudden thought?
It was obvious that the very police force which had been quoted

[1] Hobhouse, p. 86.

by Madame de Staël and the libel writers as an example: that same Machiavellian police force which obeyed the orders of a ruthless man was, in a crucial moment, seen to err through an excess of humanity. From a horror of bloodshed it lost Napoleon's family an empire. For the previous four or five months there had been plotting in Paris. But the police had despised the plotters so much that they had committed the mistake of despising the conspiracy as well.

The same thing was happening in the provinces. The Senators were well aware that certain people were corresponding with the enemy. Juries would have condemned them without a doubt, and to have brought them before the criminal courts would at least have put a stop to their machinations. However, no one wished to run the risk of bloodshed; I am able personally to vouch to the truth of this last fact.

I believe that posterity will admire Napoleon's police which, at the cost of so little bloodshed, were able to forestall so many conspiracies. During the first years which followed our Revolution; after a civil war and with a minority no less rich than it was corrupt,[1] and with a pretender who was backed by England, it is possible that a police force had been a necessary evil.[2] Look at the conduct of England in 1715 and in 1746.

The Imperial police never had cause to reproach itself with incidents such as the alleged Lyons conspiracy or the Nîmes massacres.[3]

[1] The Infernal Machine of 3 Nivôse.

[2] 'In any government not founded solely for the benefit of all by following the precepts of reason and of justice; in any government whose subjects are corrupt and who ask nothing better than to exchange rights for privileges, I am afraid that a police force is necessary.'

[3] Did the famous authoress whom I am trying to refute make her statements in all good faith? If so, then this famous woman possessed a very indifferent head. When slandering someone it is a wretched excuse to claim poor judgement. Who obliged you to speak? And if you only raised your voice to slander misfortune and to beat those already down, what is there to distinguish you from the basest of men?

The writer would be truly happy to see such reasoning destroyed. He feels the need to respect what he admires and what for so long he did respect.

It may perhaps be observed as an extenuating reason that it takes more than one kind of courage to defend the Imperial police nowadays. As for closing every

After having received the messenger, the Allies marched on Paris. Having learned of this movement a day too late, Napoleon still wanted to pursue them. But the Allies had taken the road from Meaûx, whereas Napoleon directed his army in forced marches upon Fontainebleau.

[67]

ON MARCH 29th, 160,000 ALLIED TROOPS FACED THE heights which shelter Paris to the north-east. They had left a great body of their excellent cavalry to watch Napoleon. On March 30th, at six o'clock in the morning, they opened fire from Vincennes to Montmartre. The Dukes of Ragusa and of Treviso had no more than sixteen thousand men and they held out for the whole day. They killed seven thousand of the enemy. The Paris National Guard, thirty-five thousand strong, lost one man called Fitz-James, a café owner from the Palais Royal.[1]

By five o'clock the Allies were masters of the heights of Montmartre and of Belleville; when night fell their camp fires crowned them. The capitulation had taken place in the afternoon; and the army had had to fall back on Essonne. The city, which was in fact already taken, enjoyed a very beautiful and very evil calm. The soldiers of the Guard who crossed it all through the night, wept.

[1] Other accounts say forty.

---

avenue open to criticism, that would take a profusion of words which is no part of the writer's nature. *Pauca intelligenti.* As for people who have merely interests and no opinions, they may be worthy of respect in the general run of life, but pen in hand they are always to be despised.*

Do I need to add that Bonaparte's police force, which strove to keep the legitimate king at a distance, acted so with essentially criminal intent? Yet while pursuing this wrong tack, was it cruel, and did it perpetrate or condone the commission of crimes?

For me: People from the provinces speak like judges and yet the greater part of the time they are no more than counsel.

[68]

THROUGHOUT THE WHOLE OF MARCH 30TH WHILE THE battle raged, the boulevards were a brilliant sight.

Towards nine o'clock in the morning of the 31st, there were crowds such as were customary upon bright sunny days. A good deal of fun was made of King Joseph and Count Regnault. A group of people on horseback rode by wearing white cockades and waving white handerchiefs. They cried: 'Vive le Roi!'

'Which king?' I heard the people beside me ask. No one thought of the Bourbons any more than they thought of Charlemagne. That group, which I can still see, may have consisted of some twenty persons who all looked rather worried. They were allowed to pass with the same indifference as was accorded to ordinary strollers. One of my friends who ridiculed their fear, told me that the group had assembled on the Place Louis XV and did not get beyond where the rue de Richelieu crosses the boulevards.

Towards ten o'clock, some twenty sovereigns made their entry by the Porte Saint-Denis at the head of their troops. All the balconies were full, the ladies were delighted by the spectacle. At the sight of the sovereigns they waved a mass of white handkerchiefs. Every one of them wanted to see and possibly to possess Emperor Alexander. I went up on to the balcony belonging to Nicolle, the restaurant-keeper. The ladies were admiring the pleasing appearance of the Allies and their pleasure was at its height.

So as to be able to recognize each other in the midst of so great a variety of uniforms, the allied soldiers all wore a white handkerchief tied round the left arm. The Parisians mistook it for the sash of the Bourbons and they all immediately felt royalist.

The march past of these superb troops lasted for over four hours. Nevertheless signs of royalism were only to be seen in the great square formed by the junction of the boulevards, of the rue de Richelieu, the rue Saint-Honoré and of the rue du Faubourg Saint-Honoré.

146

At five o'clock in the afternoon, M. de Maubreuil who is at present in England, attached his Medal of the Legion of Honour to his horse's ear and with the help of a rope, undertook to pull down the statue which surmounted the column in the Place Vendôme. A good many of the rabble were present and one of these people then climbed on to the column and hit the huge statue with his cane.

[69]

EMPEROR ALEXANDER STAYED AT THE HOUSE OF M. DE Talleyrand. This insignificant fact sealed the fate of France[1]; it was decisive. M . . .[2] spoke to the Emperor in the street and asked him to restore its legitimate rulers to France. The reply could not have been less definite. The same person repeated his request to several generals, also in the street. Their replies were even more unsatisfactory. No one thought of the Bourbons; no one wanted them; they were unknown. Details of a little plot should be known. Several clever people, not without daring, thought it might be possible, in the midst of all the fuss, to obtain for themselves a ministry or a gratuity. They were not hanged: they succeeded, though they received neither ministry nor gratuity.[3]

Advancing through France, the Allies were amazed; three-quarters of the time they thought that they were marching into ambush. As, unfortunately for Europe, their intelligence was not on a par with their good fortune, the Allies found themselves in the hands of the first opportunists who had the courage to go as far as their headquarters. M. de V(itrolles) was the first to arrive with letters of introduction from Abbé Scapin.[4]

---

[1] And probably of the whole of Europe from then until 1838.

[2] Stendhal had first written: Demosthène de la Rochefoucauld. A name which he then struck out, writing underneath it: 'Out of prudence three dots : M . . .' (Note by French editor.)

[3] Forgot Italy in the abdication.

[4] From caution Stendhal had disguised under this name, Abbé de Pradt. (Note by French editor.)

They both claimed to speak in the name of France and affirmed that France desired the Bourbons. The Allied generals were greatly amused by the effrontery of both these gentlemen, but however good-natured the Allies might be, they nevertheless felt such pretentions to be somewhat absurd.

M. de Talleyrand hated Napoleon who had deprived him of a ministry to which he had become accustomed. He had the good fortune to have the monarch staying in his house, who for a month was the master and legislator of France. Talleyrand employed every means to win him over and produced Abbé Scapin and other adventurers who claimed to represent the French people.

It must be admitted that these intrigues were contemptible. They only became admirable as a consequence of the terrible mistake committed two days earlier when Empress Marie-Louise and her son had been made to leave Paris. Had the Princess remained she could have offered Emperor Alexander the hospitality of the Tuileries, and Prince S(chwartzenberg) would naturally have had a deciding voice in affairs.

⌈ 70 ⌉

ON MARCH 30TH, AS HALF PARIS WENT CRAZY ON HEARING the sound of firing, the Emperor's wretched ministers, with Prince Joseph as their president, were completely at sea.

The Prince disgraced himself by giving out that he would not leave just as he was fleeing. Count Regnault-de-Saint-Jean-d'Angély brought even greater shame to him. As for the ministers, they might have stirred themselves to a certain energy since everyone looked to them and they were not devoid of intelligence; but fear of losing their positions and of being turned out by their master if they as much as let slip a word about the danger, turned them into so many Cassandras. They did not concern themselves with action but with fine writing in which the language of despotism became ever prouder the nearer the despot drew to the precipice.

On the morning of the 30th they gathered at Montmartre; the outcome of their deliberations was the bringing there of eighteen bore cannon with twelve bore shot.[1] Then, obeying the Emperor's orders, they all made for Blois. If Carnot, the Count of Lapparent, Thibaudeau, Boissy d'Anglas, the Count of Lobau and Marshal Ney had been in office they would have behaved rather differently.

[71]

AFTER THE TRIUMPHAL MARCH ALONG THE BOULEVARDS, the Emperor, the King of Prussia and Prince Schwartzenberg spent several hours on the Champs Elysées watching the march past of their troops. Then these august personages went to the house of M. de Talleyrand in the rue Saint-Florentin, near the Tuileries. In the drawing-room, they found the people we have just mentioned. Prince Schwartzenberg had authority to agree to anything. The sovereigns seemed to say that if the vast majority of the French, including the army, desired the return of the former dynasty, it would be restored to them. A council was held. It is stated that His Majesty Emperor Alexander said that to him there appeared to be three alternatives:

1. To make peace with Napoleon, after taking all suitable precautions.
2. To set up a Regency and proclaim Napoleon II.
3. To recall the Bourbons.[2]

Those who enjoyed the honour of finding themselves close to the Allied rulers argued that:
'If we have them make peace with Napoleon he will have sized

[1] It appears to me that this fact has not been proved.

[2] Later on in Alexander's statement, the *Biographie* says that he said that he would recognize and guarantee the constitution which the French nation gave to itself. According to this example and to that of the article in the capitulation of Paris relative to Ney, any nation would have been mad to have trusted in a king's promise. If Emperor Alexander had guaranteed the constitution of the Senate, there would never have arisen the state of alarm which ended quite fortuitously at Waterloo.

us up: we will remain what we are now and possibly he will have us hanged. If we have a prince recalled who has been absent for twenty years, and to whom the job will not come easily, he will make us prime ministers.'[1]

The princes were unable to realize that the virtues which filled their hearts were foreign to the French. They believed the Frenchmen's protestations in favour of their country; that sacred word with which these ambitious little men were lavish to the point of boring their illustrious listeners.

At the end of two hours' discussion: 'Well,' Emperor Alexander said, 'I declare that I will not treat any further with the Emperor Napoleon.'

Michaud the printers, who were also present at the Council of State, rushed to print the following statement which covered the walls of Paris . . .

People whom surprise had not deprived of their composure, pointed out that this poster did not exclude the King of Rome.[2] And these same seditious elements asked why no one troubled to assemble the Legislative Body which was, after all, the source of all legitimate power; and the Senate which comprised the élite of the nation and had erred not from lack of intelligence but through excessive egoism? Sixty selfish men gathered together were always more cautious than six. Furthermore, there were perhaps some ten citizens at most in the Senate. What should have been a debate was treated as a ceremony and in consequence there was the Battle of Waterloo.

If Napoleon had not dismissed the Legislative Body out of despotic caprice, none of the events which subsequently took place would have happened. If the Legislative Body on which the conduct of MM. Laîné and Flaugergues had just shed light had been reassembled, the eminently wise mind that decided the fate of France would have thought of asking its advice.

[1] The 's' is comical: they all longed to try their hand.
[2] de Pradt, p. 69.

HAVING LEARNED OF THE MOVEMENTS OF THE ENEMY, Napoleon arrived in Paris in person. At midnight on March 30th, at Essonne, half-way to Fontainebleau, he met one of the bravest generals of his Guards (General Curial) who informed him of the fatal issue of the battle.

'You behaved like cowards.'

'Sire, we were attacked by troops who outnumbered us by three to one and who were excited by the sight of Paris. Never have Your Majesty's troops fought better.'

Napoleon made no reply and ordered the horses of his carriage to be turned towards Fontainebleau. There he assembled his troops.

On April 2nd he reviewed the Army Corps of Marmont, Duke of Ragusa, who had evacuated Paris on the evening of March 31st, and who was then encamped at Essonne. This corps formed the advance guard of his army of which it constituted almost one-third. Marmont assured Napoleon of the devotion and loyalty of his men who were, in fact, above temptation; but he forgot to answer for their general. Napoleon planned to march on Paris and attack the Allies. He was deserted successively by the majority of his staff, especially by the Prince de Neuchâtel, over whose defection he jested gaily with the Duke de Bassano. Finally he held a Council of War, and for the first time he lent an ear to what Marshal Ney, the Duke of Vicenza and the most devoted members of his staff had to tell him about the general discontent which his refusal to make peace had aroused throughout France; he then abdicated in favour of his son; and on April 4th he sent Ney, MacDonald and Caulaincourt to convey this proposal to Emperor Alexander.

[73]

MARMONT[1]

WHEN THESE GENERALS PASSED THROUGH THE ADVANCE
posts of the French army and halted to have their passports
countersigned by Marmont, they told him the object of their
journey. He appeared confused and said something between his
teeth about proposals that had been made to him by Prince
Schwartzenberg, and to which it could be said that he had lent
an ear. But he added, speaking to the envoys who had been
stupefied by his words, what he had just learned altered the
whole question and he would now break off his separate negotiations. After some minutes one of the marshals broke the
silence and observed that it would be much simpler if he, Marmont, were to accompany them to Paris and join in the negotiations confided to them. Marmont actually went with them, but
with what intentions! That was what the subsequent movements
of his army corps were to reveal.

The marshals left him with Prince Schwartzenberg and went
to fulfil their mission to Alexander, who referred them to the
Senate. This sovereign had as yet no definite plan and had not
thought of the Bourbons. He had not perceived himself to be in
the hands of two intriguers, one of whom, Talleyrand, thought
mainly of avenging himself.[2]

When the officer who had accompanied the marshals to the
advance post of the army, returned to Fontainebleau and reported
that Marmont had gone with them to Paris and that he had seen
him hidden in the back of their coach, everyone expressed surprise and not a few their suspicions. But Napoleon, with his
belief in friendship, replied that if Marmont had gone with them,
he felt sure that it was so as to render him every service that lay

[1] This chapter has also been translated word for word from No. 54 of the *Edinburgh Review*. No doubt the person inculpated has a justification to make known.
[2] See the real story of the month of April 1814 told by M. de Pradt.

in his power. During the absence of the negotiators, a Council of War met at Fontainebleau comprising all the generals of the army. It was a question of deciding what they would do should the proposals set forth by the marshals be rejected. Souham, second-in-command of Marmont's Corps, was sent for like the others. Souham, who knew about Marmont's secret understanding with the enemy, feared that he would be shot upon reaching Fontainebleau, and that all had been discovered. Instead of going to Fontainebleau as he had been instructed to do, he had his Army Corps advance during the night of April 5th, until it was close to Versailles. In doing this he placed himself in the power of the Allies who occupied the town, and left the troops at Fontainebleau without any advance-posts. Souham's soldiers, unaware of the instruction which he had received, obeyed him without any misgivings. It was only on the following morning that, to their despair, they discovered into what kind of a trap they had fallen. They wanted to kill their generals and it must be admitted that they would have given the world a most beneficial example. If only one of their colonels or generals had possessed a little of this same character which had formerly been so common in the armies of the Republic, he could have killed Souham and brought the army back to Essonne.

It is pointless to add that the defection of Marmont's Army Corp at such a critical moment sealed the fate of the negotiations which had been entrusted to the Marshals. Deprived of a third of his small army, Napoleon was no longer an object of fear to the Allies. The Treaty of Fontainebleau was signed on April 11th.

We have lingered for a time over these details because Marmont's betrayal of his friend and benefactor had not been fully understood. It is neither his defence nor his surrender of Paris which deserve especial attention, but his subsequent behaviour which was to transmit his name to posterity.

[74]

THE DAY FOLLOWING THAT UPON WHICH M. DE T. (ALLEY-rand) had convinced the Allied kings that the whole of France was clamouring for the Bourbons, he went to the Senate which, weak as ever, nominated the provisional government indicated to it.

On April 2nd, the Senate deposed Napoleon; on the 3rd, the Legislative Body confirmed the acts of the Senate.

During the night of April 5th–6th, the sovereigns declared that they refused to accept Napoleon's first abdication in favour of his son. Emperor Alexander had a place of retreat offered to him and his family, with retention of his titles.[1]

[75]

LET US LEAVE NAPOLEON ON THE ISLAND OF ELBA FOR A time; events will soon recall us there.

The Provisional Government out of respect I believe for the sovereigns who had advanced wearing the white cockade, banned the tricolour cockade and proclaimed the white one.

'Good,' said Napoleon, then at Fontainebleau, 'there is a cockade all ready for my supporters, should they ever regain their courage.' The army was deeply annoyed.

This act was symbolic of the government that was to follow. The step was all the more inept in that a plausible pretext for doing away with the tricolour cockade already existed; Louis XVIII being at the time *Monsieur*, he had worn the tricolour cockade from July 11th, 1789, to June 21st, 1792.[2]

The Senate drew up a Constitution that was a contract between the nation and one man. This Constitution called Louis-

---

[1] Take a page or two and the farewell from Hobhouse.
[2] Hobhouse, Vol. I, p. 91.

Stanislas-Xavier to the throne. The prince, who was a paragon of all the virtues, arrived at Saint-Ouen. Unfortunately for us, he dared not trust in his own intelligence which was nevertheless so very superior;[1] he felt obliged to surround himself with people who knew France. Like everyone else, he had a high opinion of the abilities of the Duke of Otranto and of the Prince of Benevento. But his generosity made him forget that fidelity was not the outstanding characteristic of these men. They said to themselves:

'The King cannot possibly do without us. Let him try to govern by himself; and we will be Prime Ministers within a year.'

There remained only one alternative, which did not arise until two years later; this was that the King should find a young man of the highest ability of whom he could make a great minister.

In 1814 the corrupt man who enjoyed the King's confidence gave France the most amiable ministers she had seen for a long time. For instance, home affairs were entrusted to a man who was in himself more agreeable than all of the somewhat uncouth ministers of Napoleon and who yet firmly believed that to live in the house of the Home Secretary and to dine there was, in fact, to be Home Secretary. Throughout all its phases the Revolution had never witnessed anything so guileless as this government.[2] Had the ministers been at all energetic, they would almost certainly have done ill, as they do not appear to have been lacking in will-power. But they were impotent.[3] In his great wisdom the King groaned at the inaction of his ministers. He was so well aware of their intellectual insufficiency that he had one of them buy him the *Biographie Moderne* and he then made no appointments without first consulting the relevant biographical sketch.[4]

---

[1] What a fatuous style of writing.

[2] Who said this? Was it Hobhouse? No, I have forgotten.

[3] Staël: Vol. I, p. 127. When nations are of any importance in public affairs, all such drawing-room wits are inferior to events. It is men of principle who are needed.

[4] Said by Doligny.

[76]

WE WILL TAKE THE LIBERTY OF SPEAKING FAIRLY FREELY on the subject of some of the mistakes of this government. In the law, as well as in our heartfelt wishes, the King is inviolable and he is, above all, because his ministers are responsible. In France the King was not yet familiar with either men or events. His Government of 1818 proved what his great wisdom could achieve when it was not misled by men who guided him blindly.

Louis XVIII reached Saint-Ouen.[1] There he was purely and simply intended to accept the Constitution drawn up by the Senate. Bonaparte having, so to speak, forfeited his title of son of the Revolution through his tyranny, Louis found this an opportune moment to assume it. The procedure in question appeared at most to be purely temporary, and would not prevent a third or fourth successor, once the dangers were passed, from calling himself *King by the Grace of God*, and to speak of legitimacy. As for the King, his reign was to be happy and peaceful, with Bonaparte forever forgotten.

Abbé de Montesquiou drew up a memorandum for His Majesty in which he said, referring to the preamble to the Constitution:

'There can be no doubt but that: *King of France and of Navarre* ought to be inserted. I go so far as to think that the Constitution should be known as the King's Law.'[2]

On June 14th the Constitution was laid before both Chambers assembled in the Palace of the Legislative Body. That most amiable of ministers, the Chancellor, told the representatives of the nation:

'That several years had passed since divine Providence had called their King to the throne of his fathers . . . and that being

---

[1] What follows is a faithful translation from *The History of the Hundred Days* by J. Hobhouse.
[2] *Moniteur* of April 15th, 1814.

156

in full possession of his hereditary rights to the throne of France, he did not wish to exercise this authority which he had received from God and from his forebears other than by setting limits to his power himself . . . and that, although in France absolute power was vested in the person of the King, His Majesty wished to follow the examples of Louis-le-Gros, Philippe-le-Bel, Louis XI, Henri II, Charles IX and Louis XIV and modify the exercise of his authority.'

One must admit that Charles IX and Louis XIV were odd choices. After having expressed the desire to efface from French history everything that had taken place during his absence, the King promised faithfully to observe the charter of the Constitution, which: 'by the free exercise of royal authority he had granted and would grant, which he had conceded and would concede to his subjects'.[1]

It should be realized that in causing their sovereign to reject the Constitution of the Senate at Saint-Ouen, the King's advisers had had him make a kind of abstract of it which he then promised to grant to the people. After the entry of His Majesty, a committee was assembled at the Place Vendôme consisting of some thirty splendid minds, the most sheep-like legislators who could be found who turned this abstract into articles and drew up the charter without having any idea of what they were writing. None of the unfortunate people knew that he was privy to a transaction between the parties then dividing France. The King frequently advised them to stipulate for the faithful carrying out of all the promises contained in his Saint-Ouen proclamation. It was this haphazard Constitution that the Chancellor had placed at the beginning of the wise speech which has just been quoted.

It was in the middle of the sudden access of foolishness that had seized the capital of France, that the worthy Grégoire who had dared to advance some general principles on Liberty which were accepted by the whole of Europe, was accused by men of letters of seeking the re-birth of anarchy. MM. Lambrechts and Garat, who protested against any haste, were abused and

[1] Look up the correct terms—*To take the words in the 'Moniteur'*.

treated as metaphysicians. Benjamin Constant, the man through whom France's right-thinking is expressed, was warned to preserve a silence well suited to a foreigner uninformed as to our habits.

Ultimately this charter, so wisely prepared, was read before both the Chambers and not accepted by them. Yet they would have voted almost anything put before them, even including the Koran, for that is how things are in France. Under such circumstances, to go against the majority is to be taxed with an absurd vanity. 'In France, one must above all do as others do.' The story of the sheep of Panurge might well serve us as a coat of arms.[1]

The stupid omission of a formal acceptance of the Charter, deprived the King of all genuine legitimacy.[2] In France even schoolchildren are able to argue that every man possesses absolute and boundless power over himself of which he may transfer a part. Twenty-eight million men cannot vote, but twenty-eight million men can elect one thousand Members of Parliament to vote for them. Therefore, without a freely chosen assembly of representatives, no legitimate power can exist in France, there can only be the right of might.'[3]

[77]

THE ENTIRE CONDUCT OF THE MINISTERS WAS ON A SIMILAR level. The representatives of authority whom they had dared to depose where replaced by weak and dishonourable men. It soon became evident, not without surprise, that the Bourbon cause was daily losing adherents. The ministers committed so many follies that they convinced the people that in the depths of his heart the King was the greatest enemy of the Charter. These ministers had in their mind's eye the Court of Louis XVI

[1] *Considérations sur la Révolution*, Vol. I, p. . . . .
[2] Humorous colour to add variety: it is, moreover, the colour of the subject.
[3] *For me: is that took from Jefferson?*

and the fate of Turgot. Forever believing royal authority to be on the verge of a reawakening, and that it would understand how to reward those who had been able to foresee it while knowing how to respect it during the *days of misfortune*, the unhappy creatures thought only of vying with one another to obtain promotion.

[78]

WHATEVER MONTESQUIEU AND MANY OTHERS MAY HAVE said, there are only two kinds of government: i.e. *national* governments and *special* governments.

To the first category belong all those governments which uphold the principle that *all rights and all powers always belong to the whole body of the nation, that they are implicit in it, emanate from it and exist only by and for it.*

We shall term *special* governments all those of whatever kind they may be, which admit sources of legitimate right and power other than that of general consent, such as divine power; heredity; a tacit or deliberate social pact in which the parties make their demands as though they were powers foreign to each other.[1]

Although basically imperfect, although not even a contract between the people and one man like the English Constitution of 1688, our Charter would have satisfied everyone. The French people are too childish to examine it closely. Moreover this Charter was fairly good, and if ever it is applied, France will be fortunate, more fortunate than England. In the present century it is impossible to draw up a bad Charter; there is not one among us who could not write out an excellent one in half an hour. What would have been a supreme effort of genius in Montesquieu's times, is a commonplace nowadays. Finally, any Charter that is applied is a good charter.[2]

[1] *Commentaires sur l'Esprit des Lois* (de Destutt de Tracy), pp. 13, 14, Liège, 1817.
[2] One of Benjamin Constant's ideas.

For the throne of the wisest and best of Princes to have been shielded from any upheavals, it would have been sufficient if the people had believed the Charter to be sincerely desired. But it was precisely this idea that the clergy and the nobility did everything in their power to discourage.

A hundred thousand priests and a hundred and fifty thousand angry nobles were, like the rest of the nation, supervised by only eight idiots whose only thought was of the blue ribbon. The nobles wanted and still want to recover their estates. What could be simpler than to have given them the equivalent in Government bonds? By such means these people, who have no views but only interests, would have been tied to national credit and the Charter as to a necessary evil.

Ministers who never wrote a line or gave a dinner without infringing the spirit of the Charter had soon accumulated substantial infractions of it. Mme. la Maréchale Ney never returned from a visit to Court without tears in her eyes.[1]

[79]

1. ARTICLE 260 OF THE PENAL CODE WHICH IS UPHELD BY the Charter, forbade under penalty of imprisonment and fine, the forcing of Frenchmen to observe holidays and Sundays and to cease work. In ridiculous terms a police regulation ordered just the opposite. It laid down that all Frenchmen, whatever their religion, should *decorate the front of their houses in all streets through which the Blessed Sacrament was to pass.*

No opportunity was lost in carrying out these processions which became objects of ridicule to all parties. So long as the Roman Catholic religion has no profitable jobs to offer, it will be thought ridiculous in France. For a long time now, no one has believed in it. Religion has been forever lost in France since Abbé Maury tried to use it to shield the privileges of the nobility.

[1] Marshal Ney's interrogatory.

2. On June 10th, six days after the Charter which promised freedom of the Press (article 8), there appeared the Home Secretary's decree re-establishing censorship. What was most absurd, is that this decree was made law. For a long time, in France, the future will have no meaning for the government.

3. On June 15th, and on July 15th, two decrees on the recruiting of the Royal Guards infringed article 12 of the Charter, to the detriment of the army.

4. On June 21st and on July 6th, a Council of State was set up which, flouting article 63, was raised to the level of a special court.

5. On June 27th, article 15, the most important of them all, the one in which it is stated that the legislative power is vested in the King, the peers and in the Members of Parliament, was infringed for a mere bagatelle, by a decree annulling a tax which had been established by the law of 22nd Ventôse of the year XII.[1]

6. On December 16th unemployed officers were placed on half-pay. This was in direct opposition to article 69. This measure may have been necessary, but a law should have been passed for a period of one year, and then with misgivings, and it should have been asked for on bended knees. From that moment the army was lost to the Bourbons. In France eight men out of ten have fought at one time or another and the remaining two take pride in sharing the feelings of the army. It was at this time that the most unfortunate anecdotes began to circulate. A royal Duke asked an officer in which campaigns he had taken part: 'In all of them.' 'With what rank?' 'As the Emperor's aide-de-camp.' Backs were turned on him. To the same question another replied that he had twenty-five years' service—'twenty-five years of brigandage.' The Guards failed to please while drilling, and those old soldiers, famous for so many victories, were told that they would have to go to England to be taught their drill by the Guards of the King of England.

Swiss soldiers were brought to Paris while French soldiers

[1] Hobhouse, Vol. I, p. 63.

were placed on half-pay. Six hundred nobles, for whom the Parisians invented the name which later became so famous, of *Flying Squadron of Louis XIV*, and an equal number of children who had barely left school, were dressed in absurd costumes which had been invented by Cardinal de Richelieu, and protected the person of the King who appeared to mistrust his Guards. As soon as there exists a privileged body in Paris, one must be prepared for insolence or know how to forestall it, as Napoleon did. The scenes which took place in the Café Montansier deeply offended national vanity.

The Old Imperial Guard, that very brave and easily influenced body of men, was outrageously exiled from the capital. Marshal Soult, the Minister of War, wished to have it recalled. A countermand a thousand times more outrageous than the original order, stopped him half-way. The Chouans, who were in league with foreigners, enjoyed high favour.[1]

The Legion of Honour orphanage was closed, and what was even worse, it was then re-opened out of weakness.

The Legion of Honour was publicly sold. Moreover, it was thrown to people farthest removed from public affairs, so as to degrade it. For example, it was conferred on the scent-makers of the Palais Royal. The Bourbon army was barely eighty-four thousand strong and it was officered by five thousand old émigrés or young and beardless members of the nobility.

[80]

Here are further infringements of the Charter:

7. On July 30th a military academy was set up so that members of the nobility might enjoy the advantages of the 1751 decree.

8. On his own authority, the Chancellor imposed a tax on the *advances* which judges accorded to persons not definitely assessed; on certificates of naturalization and on newspapers.

[1] Hobhouse, Vol. I, p. 88.

9. In opposition to the letter of the Charter, the Government having been unable to pass a law for the reorganization of the Supreme Court of Appeal, renewed it by decree and dismissed several greatly respected judges; from then on all judges could be bought. In France this Court upholds the statutes of the law. It is an extremely important piece of government machinery for the maintenance of order in home administration and, up until the time to which we refer, it had been excellent.

[81]

ALTHOUGH THE PEOPLE WHO DREW UP THE CHARTER WERE unaware of it, the Charter was divided into two parts. In the first it was truly *constitutional*, that is, a recipe for the making of laws; a law on how to make laws. In the second it was a *friendly* compromise between those parties which divided France.

10. The most important of the articles of this second part is the 11th, which reads as follows: 'Any seeking after opinions and votes current up until the Restoration is forbidden.' The same oblivion was enjoined on the courts as well as on citizens.[1]

In a childish and vain people this article was one of the least important to royal authority. Those who, in France, do not enjoy favour, are always despised, and people who were protected by this article would have been the most shameless flatterers. But the ministers were quite as childish as the rest of the nation. They very much wanted to obtain the dismissal of certain members of the Supreme Court of Appeal. In the palaces of kings one always tries to be ahead of the opinion attributed to the sovereign.[2]

[1] See the so-called law of *amnesty* which sent into exile all who had voted for the death of Louis XVI.
[2] Freedom of the Press was disliked, but people were too weak to prevent it. The appearance of defying the government lent a certain piquancy to the review *Le Nain Jaune* and what . . .*

*The end of this note was cut when the MS. was bound.

11. Another even more incomprehensible piece of foolishness. to anyone unfamiliar with the leaders of the period, was the dismissal of fifteen members of the Institut. This exceedingly ridiculous *coup d'état* gained importance from its consequences It was a blow to the nation, almost the last straw. The next day, had it been able to do so, the French people would have hounded out the Bourbons. Yet what did it matter either to the Bourbons or to the French people whether the following belonged to the Institut: Guyton-Morveau; Carnot; Monge; Napoleon Bonaparte; Cambacérès; Merlin; Roederer, Garat, Sieyès, Cardinal Maury; Lucien Bonaparte, Lakanal, Grégoire, Joseph Bonaparte and David?

What is unbelievable is that names were found to replace those which had been eliminated. There were people who agreed to enter, *by decree*, a body which only owed its importance to public opinion. In the days of d'Alembert and of Duclos, it would not have been so. And then people are surprised that men of letters constitute the most degraded class in Paris.[1]

[82]

THE MANNER IN WHICH THE LEGISLATIVE BODY WAS selected under Napoleon is common knowledge. The Senators merely nominated their cook's *protégés*. Nevertheless, such was the energy which the *cult of glory* inspired in the nation, such was its contempt for pettiness, that no Chamber appointed during the Restoration Empire won for itself so great an esteem as that in which MM. Durbach, Lainé, Bedoch, Raynouard, Suard and Flaugergues shone. The speeches of these worthy persons comforted the nation. At that time everything connected with the government was degraded.

[1] Which explains why decent people dislike becoming authors and putting their names to the titles of their books.

I have counted eleven infringements of the Charter. But I believe that the *Edinburgh Review* accounts for fourteen or fifteen.

The real royalists, the die-hards, the *émigrés* affected to smile disdainfully at the words *charter* and *liberal ideas*. They forgot that the man who had set them on their feet, the magnanimous Alexander, had advised the Senate to give France *strong and liberal institutions*. A thousand sinister rumours announced to the nation on every hand the forthcoming resurrection of the *Ancien Régime*.

The most popular ministers, MM. D(ambray) F(errand), M(ontesquiou), B(lacas) missed no opportunity of professing the doctrine of absolute monarchy. They openly regretted the Old France in which without exception the blessed words *Dieu et le Roi*[1] had been entwined in every heart.

Rest assured that the equally sacred rights of the *faithful nobility* were not overlooked. Possibly not everyone remembers that these rights consisted of one hundred and forty-four taxes, all of them different.[2] Finally, the Duke of Feltre, the Minister of War who did not even enjoy the fame of military achievements, dared to say when addressing the Chamber:

'If the King wills it the law wills it', and he became a marshal. Finally, although no one would believe it, M. de Chateaubriand did not appear to be sufficiently royalist; and his reply to General Carnot's memorandum was attacked in this sense.[3]

[83]

ON JUNE 4TH MEMBERS OF THE OLD PARLIAMENT HAD MET at the house of M. Lepelletier de Morfontaine[4] and had formerly protested against the charter. They had also received the treatment accorded to all minorities: 'Either you submit to the law or get out.'[5] No one appeared to take any notice of this absurd

---

[1] Address from the Paris clergy to the King, August 15th, 1814.
[2] And several of which joined a contempt for the human race to . . .
[3] *Journal des Débats*, October.
[4] Translated literally from J. Hobhouse, Vol. I, p. 96, 2nd ed.
[5] Paley.

protest and the nobility immediately prepared to make a similar one.

In France, where everyone aspires to form a regiment so as to become a colonel, such proceedings as these have their importance. They are the country's conspiracies. A political ruler would have punished them severely.

At Savenay in the Loire-Inférieure on March 5th, a sermon was preached. The faithful were told that those who did not return their property to the nobles and to the priests as representatives of the monks, would suffer the fate of Jezebel, and be eaten by dogs.

Among the petitions which the Legislative Body refused to read, were to be found nearly three hundred from individuals who complained that their *curés* had refused them absolution because they owned national property. Now some eight million Frenchmen were in the same boat, and they were precisely the eight million who possessed the most energy. In October, newspapers belonging to the Court reported that at a party which the Prince of Neuchâtel had given at Grosbois for the King and the Royal Family, the Prince had paid homage to His Majesty by giving him a roll of parchment which contained the deeds of ownership to this national property. The King had kept the deeds for an hour and had then returned them to the marshal with the gracious words: 'These title-deeds cannot be in better hands.' Berthier protested to the King at this ridiculous story and, what I am far from believing, he was never able to get permission to have it denied in the newspapers.

M. Ferrand proposed a very just law: the question of restoring their unsold property to the *émigrés*.[1]

He dared to speak in the tribune of 'the sacred and inviolable rights which those who had always followed the straight and narrow path had to estates of which they had been stripped by the storms of the Revolution', and M. Ferrand later received the blue ribbon of the order of the Saint-Esprit.

[1] Moreover, the émigrés were to have restored to them up to a maximum of 6,000 francs income *per capita* and in *State Bonds* all that had been taken from them at the precise moment when they had left France to call foreigners into the country.

This speech enflamed France. People who lived peacefully and submissively under the rule of the Dey of Algiers, waxed furious at any covert remark that contained a threat to their estates.

[84]

It is time to return to the island of Elba. Having read in a newspaper while shaving the speech of Minister Ferrand, Napoleon sent for General Bertrand and told him: . . .

[85]

Baron Jermanovski, Colonel of the Guards Lancers, gave the following account to his good friend General Kosciusko.[1] It was gallantry speaking in the presence of heroism.

The colonel began by saying that his command was at Porto Longone where beside his lancers he had a garrison of three hundred infantrymen. Six days before leaving, the Emperor had sent for him to inquire the number of ships in his harbour. He received orders to charter them, to provision them and to prevent the departure of the most insignificant ship. The day before the embarkation he received orders to pay three thousand francs for a road Napoleon was having built. He had almost forgotten the embargo when on February 26th, while he was working in his small garden, one of the aides-de-camp to the Emperor brought him the order to embark all his men at six o'clock that evening and to rejoin the flotilla off Porto Ferraio the same night at the appointed hour. It was so late that the colonel was unable to finish embarking his men before seven-thirty. They left immediately. With his little fleet he reached the brig *Inconstant* which was already under sail. On mounting to the deck he found the Emperor who greeted him with the questions: 'How goes it? Where are all your people?'

[1] Hobhouse, p. 115. See the accounts in the *Moniteur*, which are correct.

Colonel Jermanovski learned from his colleagues that the garrison of Porto Ferraio had only received orders to embark that same day at one o'clock and that they had come aboard only at four o'clock. The Emperor with Generals Bertrand and Drouot and his staff had arrived at eight o'clock and that then a single cannon-shot had given the signal and they had set sail. The flotilla consisted of the *Inconstant* with twenty-six guns, the *Etoile* and the *Caroline* bombardes, and four feluccas. On board the *Inconstant* were four hundred men of the Old Guard. No one knew where they were going. The Old Grenadiers upon leaving shore to go on board had cried: 'Paris or death.'

The wind, which had been in the south and rather strong at first, soon dropped to a flat calm. When day dawned they had done no more than six leagues and the flotilla found itself between the islands of Elba and of Capraia in sight of English and French cruisers. Nevertheless the night had not been wholly lost as the soldiers and crew had been engaged in altering the colour of the hulk of the brig from yellow and grey to black and white. This was a wretched way in which to escape the observation of those interested in watching the Island of Elba.

The question arose of putting back into Porto Ferraio, but Napoleon ordered them to continue on their way, determined, should the need arise, to attack the French cruisers. In the waters around Elba there were two frigates and one brig. In fact it was thought that they would be more disposed to come and join the Imperial fleet than to fight against it. But any fairly determined royalist officer could have had the first shot fired and carried his crew with him. At noon the wind freshened; by four o'clock the flotilla was standing off Leghorn. They sighted three warships and one of them, a brig, sailed towards the *Inconstant*. The portholes were closed. The soldiers of the Guard removed their shakos and lay down on the deck. The Emperor planned to try and board the brig, though only as a last resource, in case the royal ship refused to allow the *Inconstant* to continue on her way without visiting her. The *Zéphir*, which was the name of the brig flying the white pennant, came full sail towards the

Inconstant, and the two vessels passed deck to deck. Captain Andrieux[1] having been hailed by Lieutenant Taillade of the *Inconstant* who was a friend of his, contented himself with inquiring the *Inconstant's* destination. 'To Genoa', replied Taillade and he added that he would be glad to execute any commissions for him which he might desire. Andrieux replied in the negative, and in parting called out: 'How is the Emperor?' To which Napoleon replied: 'Wonderfully well', and the two ships drew apart.

The wind increased during the night of the 27th, and on February 28th,[2] at daybreak, they had a glimpse of the coast of Provence. They caught sight of a seventy-four-gun vessel that was apparently sailing to Sardinia.[3] Colonel Jermanovski said that up to that moment it had been generally believed on board that they were on their way to Naples. Many questions were put to the officers by the men and even by officers to the Emperor, who made no reply. Then finally he said smiling: 'Well, it is France!' At these words everyone crowded round him to hear his instructions. The first measure which he undertook was to order two or three of the commissaires of his little army to make ready their pens and papers. At his dictation they wrote the proclamations to the army and to the French people. When they had been written they were read aloud. Napoleon made several alterations. He then had them re-read and once again corrected them. Finally, after at least ten different versions had been made, he said: 'That's good, make copies of them.' At these words all the soldiers and sailors who could write lay down on the deck. Paper was issued to them, and they had soon made a sufficient number of copies of the proclamation for them to be published at the time of the landing. They then busied themselves making tricolour cockades. They only had to tear off the outer edge of the cockade of the Island of Elba. At first, upon reaching the island, the Emperor's cockade had even more

[1] See the *Biographie.*
[2] To be verified in Hobhouse, whether the 28th or the 1st March.
[3] Is this 'tour' right? Doesn't he mean leaving?

closely resembled the French one. He subsequently had it changed so as not to arouse suspicion. During these various arrangements, and in general throughout the latter part of the voyage, the officers, soldiers and sailors surrounded Napoleon, who slept little and remained almost always on deck. Lying down, sitting, standing or strolling familiarly around him they felt the need of talking to him. They asked incessant questions, to which he replied without the least sign of impatience, although several were not a little indiscreet. They wanted to know his opinion on several important and still living personages, on the kings, marshals and ministers of the past. They undertook to discuss with him certain well-known passages[1] of his own campaigns and even of his domestic policy. He knew how to satisfy or how to elucidate their curiosity and frequently entered into great detail on the subject of his own conduct and that of his enemies. Whether he examined his contemporaries' claims to fame or whether he recalled the military facts of ancient and modern times, all his answers were expressed in an easy tone,[2] of noble frankness and a familiarity which delighted the soldiers. 'Every word', said Colonel Jermanovski, 'seemed to us worthy to be preserved for posterity.' The Emperor spoke unreservedly of his present undertaking, of the difficulties it offered and of his hopes. 'In such a case as this,' he said, 'one must think slowly but act quickly. For long I weighed the idea; I examined it with all the attention of which I was capable. I have no need to tell you of the deathless glory and the advantages that shall be ours if our undertaking is crowned by success. If we fail, it is not to soldiers who since childhood have braved death in all its forms and in so many climates that I shall attempt to disguise the fate that awaits us. We know it and we despise it.'

Such were almost the last words he spoke before his little fleet dropped anchor in Golfe Juan. Those last words had an air of having been more prepared. It was as though it were a kind

---

[1] Instead of passages, perhaps epochs.
[2] Is this French. Etre d'un ton *pour* avoir un ton d'aisance ? Look it up in J-J.

of address to his companions to whom perhaps he would not have time to speak in the midst of the hazards they were about to affront.

On February 28th, Antibes had been in sight since noon and on March 1st, at three o'clock in the afternoon, the fleet dropped anchor in the bay. A captain and twenty-five men were sent to capture any battery which conceivably might dominate the landing-place. Finding that there were no batteries, the officer on his own initiative marched into Antibes. He entered the town and was taken prisoner. At five o'clock the troops landed on the shore nearest to Cannes. The Emperor was the last to leave the ship. He rested for a time in a bivouac that had been prepared for him in a small meadow among the olive trees, close by the sea. Nowadays peasants show visitors the little table on which he ate his meal![1]

The Emperor sent for Jermanovski and asked if he knew how many horses had been brought from Elba. The Colonel replied that he knew nothing about them and that so far as he was concerned, he had not embarked a single horse.

'Well,' said Napoleon, 'I brought four horses. Let us divide them. I think that I should have one. Since you command my cavalry you will need the second, Bertrand, Drouot and Cambronne must share the remaining two.'

The horses had been landed a little farther down on the beach. They left the army, and accompanied by his staff, Napoleon went on foot to where they were to be found. The Emperor walked by himself, interrogating a few peasants he met. Jermanovski and the generals followed, carrying their saddles. When they reached the horses, Grand Marshal Bertrand refused to take one. He said that he would walk. Drouot did the same. Cambronne and Molat each mounted a horse. The Emperor gave Colonel Jermanovski a handful of napoleons and told him to get some horses from the peasants. The colonel gave the peasants whatever they asked and bought fifteen beasts. They were harnessed to the three pieces of cannon

[1] December 27th, 1819. Hobhouse.

brought from Elba and to another cannon which Princess Pauline had given to her brother.

Someone came to tell of the ill-fortune of Antibes. 'We have begun badly,' said the Emperor, 'now we have nothing better to do than to march as fast as we can and take the mountain passes before news of our landing reaches that far.' The moon rose and Napoleon with his little army set out at eleven o'clock. They marched all night. The peasants in the villages through which they passed remained silent. They shrugged their shoulders and shook their heads when told that the Emperor had returned from Elba. At Grasse, a town of six thousand inhabitants through which the Emperor passed, it was believed that pirates had landed and everything was in a state of alarm. Shops and windows were closed, and the crowds gathered in the streets, despite the national cockades and the cries of *Long live the Emperor* from the soldiers, let them pass without giving the least sign of approval or of disapproval. They rested for an hour on a slope outside the town. The soldiers began to look at one another with uncertainty and sadness. All of a sudden they saw a troop of people from the town coming towards them bearing food and crying *Long live the Emperor!*

From then on the peasants showed themselves glad that Napoleon had landed, and his progress was more of a triumph than an invasion. The cannons and the coach were left at Grasse, and since the roads were very bad, in the course of their first march, which was of twenty-five leagues, Napoleon frequently went on foot in the midst of his Grenadiers. When they complained of being tired, he called them his *grumblers* and they on their side, whenever he chanced to stumble, would laugh aloud at his clumsiness. The evening of the 2nd they reached the village of Seranon, twenty leagues from Grasse. During this march, among the soldiers Napoleon's names were: *notre petit tondu* and *Jean de l'épée*. Napoleon would often hear these names repeated in a subdued voice as he climbed the ascent in the midst of his veterans. On the 3rd he slept at Barrème, and dined at Digne, on March 4th. 'It was either at Digne or at

Castellane', the colonel tells us, 'that Napoleon undertook to make the owner of the inn in which he was staying cry: *Long live the Emperor*. This the man resolutely refused to do and cried instead: *Long live the King*. Instead of being angry, Napoleon praised him for his loyalty and only asked him to drink his health, to which mine host agreed most willingly.'

At Digne the proclamations[1] to the army and to the French people were printed and distributed in the Dauphiné along the route he followed with such speed that Napoleon found towns and villages all ready to welcome him. Up to that time, however, he had only been joined by one recruit. This soldier had been met on the road by Colonel Jermanovski, who undertook to convert him. When the colonel told him that the Emperor was about to arrive, the soldier began to laugh with all his heart: 'Good,' he said, 'now I shall have something to tell them at home this evening.' The colonel had great difficulty in persuading him that he was not joking. Then the soldier asked: 'Where do you intend sleeping tonight?' and upon learning the name of the village, 'Very well,' he replied, 'my mother lives three leagues from this place, I am going to say good-bye to her and I will be with you this evening.' In effect, that very evening the grenadier clapped the colonel on the shoulder, and was only satisfied when he was sure that the colonel would tell the Emperor that Grenadier Melon had come to share the fortunes of his former master.

Napoleon spent the night of March 5th at Gap where he was guarded by only ten horsemen and forty grenadiers. The same day General Cambronne with forty grenadiers occupied the bridge and ancient fortress of Sisteron,[2] but Melon remained the only recruit to have been made, so that at Saint-Bonnet and in other villages the inhabitants wanted to ring the tocsin and rise *en masse* to accompany the little army. They obstructed the roads and frequently impeded the advance of the army so as to see the Emperor who occasionally went on foot.

[1] Hobhouse.
[2] Hobhouse.

The roads were terrible on account of the melting snows. A pack-mule loaded with gold slipped over a precipice. The Emperor appeared to be much put out about it. Two hours were spent trying to pull the mule out. Finally, so as not to lose any more time, the Emperor was forced to leave it behind. The peasants benefited by it in the spring.

On March 6th the Emperor slept at Gap, and General Cambronne and his advance-guard of forty men at La Mure. There the outpost of the Grenoble garrison, six hundred strong, refused to parley with General Cambronne. Colonel Jermanovski, who was at the head of the advance guard, found a mountain pass near Vizille which was occupied by troops which carried the white flag of the Bourbons. He wanted to speak, but an officer advanced towards him calling out 'Withdraw, I can have no communication with you. Keep your distance or my men will open fire.' The colonel tried to win him over by telling him that he would have to speak with Emperor Napoleon and not with him, but the officer continued to proffer threats and Jermanovski went to tell Napoleon of his lack of success. Napoleon said to him with a smile: 'If that is so, I shall have to see what I can do about it.' He dismounted and ordered some fifty of his grenadiers to follow him with arms reversed. He walked quietly to the pass where he found a battalion of the 5th of the Line, a company of sappers and one of the Engineer Corps, some seven or eight hundred men in all. The commanding officer continued to shout, frequently at the Emperor himself, saying: 'It's an impostor, it is not he.' From time to time this same officer would reprimand his troops and order them to open fire. When they saw Napoleon's men advancing, it looked for a time as though they wished to sight their rifles. Napoloen made his grenadiers halt, and then went quietly and all by himself up to the battalion. When he was quite close to the front line, he stopped short, looked at them calmly and then opening his *redingote* shouted to them: 'Look, it is I, don't you recognize me? If there is one soldier among you who wishes to kill his Emperor let him fire, for now is the moment.'

They were beaten in a second and in midst of redoubled cries of *Long live the Emperor*, they flung themselves into the arms of the Guards.

Shortly before the soldiers of the Fifth broke up Napoleon approached a grenadier who had his rifle at the ready and, taking hold of one of his moustaches he said: 'And you, old Moustache, were you not with us at Marengo?'

That is a simple account of one of those actions which in every century and in every country show nations who are the men for whom they should march and act.

Napoleon's companions considered the actions of this troop of seven hundred men to have been decisive. They saw in this incident that the Emperor had not been mistaken and that the army was still for him.[1] The new troops donned the tricolour cockade, grouped themselves around the Eagles of the Army of Elba and in their company entered Vizille to the joyful acclamations of its inhabitants. This small market town has always been known for its patriotism. It may be said that it was there that the French Revolution and world freedom began. It was at the Château de Vizille that the first meeting of the Etats du Dauphiné was held.

While proceeding towards Grenoble, Colonel Jermanovski was joined by an officer who came up to him at full speed and said: 'Permit me to salute you in the name of Colonel Charles Labédoyère.'

This young colonel soon appeared at the head of the greater part of his regiment, the Seventh of the Line, made up from the remains of the 112th Regiment and several others. At four in the afternoon, the colonel had escaped from Grenoble, when he was some distance away he pulled an eagle from his pocket, placed it on the end of a pole and kissed it in front of his regiment who instantly shouted *Long live the Emperor!* He then stuck a knife into a drum filled with tricolour cockades which he distributed to his regiment. However, General Marchand who remained loyal to the King, succeeded in making part of the regiment

[1] Hobhouse, p. 128.

return to Grenoble. In the town the garrison had been increased by the Eleventh Regiment of the Line and part of the Seventh, which had been sent on from Chambéry. This garrison was, moreover, composed of two thousand men of the Third Pioneer Regiment, of two battalions of the Fifth of the Line and of the Fourth Artillery Regiment, precisely the very regiment in which, twenty-five years before, Napoleon had been given command of a company.

Grenoble is a poorly fortified town that is maintained solely to provide artillery for the chain of the Alps, in the middle of which the town lies. On the side of the town overlooking the plain there is only a wall, rising in terraces twenty feet high, with a small stream flowing in front of it. It was with such absurd fortifications as these that, a few months later on their own initiative, the inhabitants of Grenoble killed one thousand two hundred men of the Piedmontese army, consisting entirely of Napoleon's soldiers.

When the great man approached the town on March 7th, the whole garrison was drawn up on the terraced ramparts, in the centre of which is the Roman Gate which faces the road of Vizille,[1] the guns were loaded, the fuses lit and the National Guard, placed behind the garrison troops, acted as reserve.

The Porte de Bonne was closed at half-past eight. As Napoleon entered the little suburb of Saint-Joseph, Colonel Jermanovski accompanied by eight Polish Lancers appeared before the Porte de Bonne and demanded the keys. He was told that General Marchand had them. The colonel spoke to the soldiers who remained silent. Napoleon soon appeared on the little bridge outside the Gate. He remained there for more than three-quarters of an hour, seated on a guard-stone.

General Marchand should have gone out on to a nearby rampart, fifty feet at most from the Emperor's person, and shot him himself. He could have been seconded by twenty gentlemen. It would have been impossible to have missed. With Napoleon dead everyone would have abandoned the cause. If the men had

[1] Hobhouse.

176

felt that it was ill-timed for them to be cut to pieces while firing they could have taken up positions in the house of a certain Eymar which gave on to the ramparts on one side, and on the other on to that part of the walls enclosed by the barracks. The truth is that at this critical moment any daring plan would have met with success. It would have been equally easy for twenty gentlemen to have been placed in the houses in the suburb of Saint-Joseph where Napoleon would have passed within fifteen feet of them.

After three-quarters of an hour of negotiations and uncertainty, instead of opening fire the garrison shouted: *Long live the Emperor!* When the gates failed to open, the people of the suburb brought beams of wood and with the help of the townspeople demolished the Gate which proved to be very strong, Grenoble having been on the point of having to sustain a siege a year previously. As the Gate fell, the keys were brought. Upon entering the town the eight Polish Lancers met a crowd of inhabitants carrying flaming torches, rushing to meet Napoleon. A moment later he entered the town alone and on foot, twenty paces in front of those who accompanied him.

Several far-seeing officers had left Grenoble and gone to meet Napoleon. If he had been unsuccessful at the Porte de Bonne, they had made all preparations for him to have crossed the Isère close by the Porte Saint-Laurent which lies at the foot of the mountain. On this mountain known as La Bastille, the ramparts were no more than an ordinary half tumbledown garden wall.

These officers advised the Emperor to prevent his soldiers from firing even one shot, as it would give an appearance of being 'defeated people' to those who joined him. Possibly half the army might have held out as a matter of honour.

The crowd surrounded him. They stared at him, grabbed his hands and knees, kissed his garments, or at least strove to touch them. Nothing could curb their enthusiasm. Napoleon did not merely represent his own government, but a government that was opposed to that of the Bourbons. They wanted him to

177

stay at the Town Hall, but he chose instead to stay at an inn kept by a former soldier of his army of Egypt, by name M. Labarre. There his staff completely lost sight of him. At the end of half an hour Jermanovski and Bertrand finally succeeded, by using all their strength, in forcing their way into the room where they found Napoleon surrounded by people who appeared completely demented, in as much as enthusiasm and affection had caused them to forget the most elementary precautions usually taken to avoid suffocating people. His officers succeeded in emptying the room for a time: they piled tabled and chairs against the door to prevent a second invasion, but in vain. The mob succeeded in pushing its way in again and for two hours the Emperor was lost in their midst, without a single soldier to protect him. He could have been killed a thousand times over if, among the priests and royalists there had been one man of courage. Shortly afterwards, the crowd brought the gates of the Porte de Bonne beneath the window of his inn shouting, 'Napoleon, we were unable to offer you the keys of your good city of Grenoble, but here are its gates'.

The next day Napoleon reviewed troops on the parade ground. There he was once more surrounded by the people. Enthusiasm had reached its highest pitch, yet it inspired none of the obsequiousness with which people are accustomed to approach kings. They shouted incessantly beneath his window as well as around him: 'No more conscription, we won't have it any longer, we need a constitution.' A young man of Grenoble (M. Joseph Rey) collected the views of the people and turned them into an address to Napoleon.

A young glove-maker, M. Dumoulin, to whose house two days before a man of Grenoble returning from Elba, a surgeon to the Emperor, had come seeking asylum, offered the Emperor his person and one hundred thousand francs. Napoleon told him: 'I do not need money at present. I thank you. What I do need is people of determination.'

The Emperor made the glove-maker an aide-de-camp and at once confided a mission to him of which the young man acquitted himself extremely well. Then and there this young man abandoned a flourishing business.

Napoleon received the public authorities. He spoke to them at length, but his arguments were too exalted to be grasped by people who for fourteen successive years had grown accustomed to being ruled by a rod of iron and to cherish no other feeling than fear of losing their stipends. They listened to Napoleon with an expression of stupidity, and he was never able to extract a single sincere remark from them. The peasants and the lower middle classes were his real friends. Their words breathed an heroic patriotism. In an address printed in Grenoble, Napoleon thanked the people of the Dauphiné. Almost all the soldiers had their tricolour cockades hidden in their shakos; they wore it once again with unutterable joy. General Bertrand, who carried out the duties of chief-of-staff, ordered the Grenoble garrison to proceed to Lyons.

On the road from Grenoble to Lyons, for the greater part of the way, Napoleon travelled without a single soldier at his side. Since the peasants filled the road, his carriage was frequently forced to go at a walking pace. They all wanted to speak to him, to touch him or at the very least to see him. They climbed on to his carriage, on to the horses that drew it, and pelted him from every side with bunches of violets and primroses. In a word, Napoleon was constantly enveloped in the arms of the people.

In the evening near Rives, the peasants walked beside him for more than a mile, lighting him on his way with hastily improvised torches, singing a song which in two months had spread like wildfire, and was of such a kind that priests, before granting absolution, asked those whom they confessed if they had sung it, and in the case of the answer being in the affirmative, they would refuse to reconcile them with God.[1]

At the village of Rives, Napoleon was not recognized just at

[1] Insert here the song, in bad French, which would appear to have been composed for the peasants and which expressed above all hatred and scorn for those who had betrayed him. Among those named in it were Augereau, Marmont and Marchand.

first. But when they realized who he was, the peasants swamped the inn and seeing that his supper was far from good, they competed with each other to bring him something to eat.

On March 9th, the Emperor spent the night at Bourgoin. Sometimes his carriage was preceded by a half a dozen hussars, but generally there was no one, and he was always three or four miles in front of the army. The Grenadiers from Elba who, worn out, had remained in Grenoble, soon wished to leave, but the most diligent among them only reached Bourgoin an hour after Napoleon had left, which gave them ample excuse to swear. They told the peasants the most insignificant details of the Emperor's life on the island of Elba. After the mutual enthusiasm, the most striking characteristic in the relationship between the soldiers and peasants was this, seeing that the uniforms and shakos of the soldiers were torn and clumsily cobbled up the peasants said: 'So the Emperor didn't have any money on Elba, since you are so badly turned out?'

'Ho! He had no lack of money since he built, made roads and changed the whole country. When he saw us looking sad, he would say to us: "Well, grumbler, so you are still hankering after France?"

' "Sire, it means that I'm bored."

' "Then get busy and mend your uniform. We have some all ready in the stores. You won't always be bored." And, said the Grenadiers, he himself set the example, his hat was all mended. We could see quite plainly that he had it in mind to lead us somewhere, but he didn't want to say anything definite. We were always being embarked and disembarked so as to mislead the people of the island.'

The Emperor had his hat repaired at Grenoble where he could easily have bought another one. The Emperor had a very worn grey redingote buttoned from top to bottom. He was so fat and tired that frequently, when getting into his carriage, his legs had to be lifted in. This led the gentlemen of the village to conclude that perhaps he was putting on a show.

On the other side of La Verpillère the carriage found itself brought to a standstill without there being any guards or crowds of peasants. Napoleon went up to the carriage of a tradesman which was also at a standstill . , .[1]

[86]

Democracy or despotism are on the first forms of government to confront mankind as it emerges from a state of savagery. This is the first stage of civilization. Aristocracy under one or more leaders—and the kingdom of France prior to 1789 was nothing more than a religious and military aristocracy of gown and sword—aristocracy under whatever name has everywhere replaced these inchoate forms of government. This is the second stage of civilization. Representative government under one or more leaders is a new, a very new invention which shapes and establishes a third stage of civilization. This sublime invention which is a tardy, albeit a necessary, product of the discovery of printing, is subsequent to Montesquieu.

Napoleon was the finest product of the second stage of civilization. It is therefore highly absurd on the part of kings who seek to remain at this second stage of civilization, to allow their scurrilous writers to attack this great man. Napoleon never understood the third stage of civilization. Where would he have studied it? Certainly not at the Academy of Brienne. Books on philosophy or translations from the English do not penetrate into royal schools, and since leaving school he had had no time for reading; he had only had time to study mankind.

Napoleon is, therefore, a nineteenth-century tyrant. Whoever says tyrant says superior mind, and it is impossible for an outstanding genius not to absorb, almost unwittingly, the good sense that fills the air.

One should read the life of Castruccio Castracani, the four-

[1] Projected crossing at Miribelle. Heavily laden waggons: no accident. Accident for the Count d'Artois.

teenth-century tyrant[1] of Lucca, so as firmly to grasp this point of view. The resemblance between the two men is striking. It is curious to follow in Napoleon's soul the fight between the genius of tyranny and the profound reasoning powers which had made a great man of him. One should have witnessed his natural inclination towards the nobility contending with the waves of contempt that rose to his eyes as soon as he observed them closely. It is clearly to be felt that in all his acts against them, his anger was that of a father. To those worthy people who may have some doubts on this subject, we would point to his rage against all that was truly liberal. This hatred would have become a frenzy had Napoleon been unaware of his strength. One should have seen how well aware his foxy courtiers were of this nuance in the master's character. From this point of view his ministers' reports make curious reading. In incidental phrases or, better, in adjectives and adverbs is to be found an entire policy governing a behaviour inspired by the most petty and cowardly tyranny. No one as yet dared to risk any such thing in the direct meaning of a sentence. An impertinent attributive adjective would reveal to the master his minister's heart. A few years more and his devoted assessors would have given him a generation of ministers who, not having gained their experience of affairs under the Republic, would merely have blushed at being inadequate courtiers. When one sees the consequences of this one comes almost to rejoice at the fall of Napoleon.

The great man's fight against the heart of a tyrant may be seen even better during his reign of a hundred days. He sent for Benjamin Constant and for Sismondi. He listened to them with apparent enjoyment, yet he soon returned enthusiastically to the cowardly councils of Regnault de Saint-Jean d'Angély and the Duke of Bassano. Such men show to what an extent he had already been corrupted by tyranny. At the time of Marengo he would have repulsed them with scorn.

These two men destroyed Napoleon far more than did the

[1] In Machiavelli and better still in the original writers abridged by Pignotti.

Battle of Waterloo. Yet no one can say that he lacked advice. At Lyons I saw one of his officers advise him in writing to abolish at a stroke both the new and the old nobility. It was Regnault, I believe, who advised him to call his new constitution the *Acte additionnel.* In the course of a single morning he lost the hearts of ten million Frenchmen, and of the only ten millions able to fight and to think. From then on those around him saw that his ruin was inevitable. How were the eleven hundred thousand soldiers advancing on France to be defeated? What he required was a political conjuring trick with the House of Austria and in proportion to the way in which he avoided men of ability, the allies welcomed them to their councils.

His justifications which come from Saint Helena strive to excuse him on the grounds of the extreme mediocrity of members of his family. Talent is never lacking, it bursts forth in quantity when it is needed. In the first place he had banished Lucien. He had made insufficient use of Soult, Lezay-Marnezia, of Levoyer d'Argenson, Thibaudeau, Count de Lapparent, Jean de Bry and of a thousand others who would have come forward. Who had any idea of the ability of Count Decazes in the days of the Emperor? The misfortunes of his family are therefore a poor excuse. Napoleon had no men of ability because he wanted none. The mere presence of Regnault sufficed to discourage all that was good.

It is fortunate for all these people that they should have had such successors.[1]

[87]

WE HAVE SHOWN NAPOLEON POSSESSED OF THOSE CHAR-acteristics which appear to us to result from the most faithful accounts; we ourselves spent several years at his court.

He was a man with amazing abilities and a dangerous ambition; by his talents the finest man to have appeared since

[1] Adequate. But the style is cold and hard.

Caesar, whom in our eyes he would appear to have surpassed. He was born to endure adversity with firmness and majesty rather than to know prosperity without allowing it to go to his head. Carried away to the verge of frenzy when his passions met with opposition, yet more susceptible to friendship than to an enduring hatred, tainted by some of the essential vices of a conqueror, yet no more prodigal of blood, no more indifferent to humanity than men like Caesar, Alexander or Frederick the Great, to whom he will be compared and whose fame will diminish daily. Napoleon was engaged in many wars which shed torrents of blood, but in none of them, with the exception of the war in Spain, was he the aggressor. He had been on the point of transforming the European continent into one vast monarchy. This plan, if it ever existed, is his sole excuse for not having revolutionized those states which he had conquered, and for having failed to turn them into moral supports for France, by making them follow the same moral road. Succeeding generations will say that it was by resisting the attacks of his neighbours that he increased his Empire.

'In raising wars for me,' he said, 'circumstances gave me the means to extend my Empire, and I did not fail to take advantage of them.'

His greatness of soul in misfortune and his renunciation have been equalled by some, but surpassed by none. Mr. Warden bears frequent witness to these qualities and we may add that they were devoid of any ostentation. The manner in which he lived at Saint Helena was completely unaffected. In modern times it is perhaps this which puts us most in mind of Plutarch. To one of those who visited him at Elba and who expressed surprise at the admirable calm with which he endured his change of fortune, he replied:

'It is because I think everybody was more surprised than I. I have no very high opinion of mankind and I have always mistrusted good fortune. Moreover, I have known little enjoyment: my brothers have been far more kingly than I. They had all the pleasures of royalty; I have known almost nothing but its weariness.'